THE POLICE
AND CRIMINAL EVIDENCE
ACT 1984
First Supplement to the Fifth Edition

AUSTRALIA
Law Book Co.
Sydney

CANADA and USA
Carswell
Toronto

HONG KONG
Sweet & Maxwell Asia

NEW ZEALAND
Brookers
Wellington

SINGAPORE and MALAYSIA
Sweet & Maxwell Asia
Singapore and Kuala Lumpur

THE POLICE
AND CRIMINAL EVIDENCE
ACT 1984
(First Supplement to the Fifth Edition)

BY

MICHAEL ZANDER Q.C.
Emeritus Professor, London School of Economics
and Political Science

THOMSON

TM

SWEET & MAXWELL

Published in 2006 by
Sweet & Maxwell Limited
100 Avenue Road
Swiss Cottage
London NW3 3PF
www.sweetandmaxwell.co.uk

Typeset by J&L Composition, Filey, North Yorkshire
Printed by Athenaeum Press Ltd, Gateshead, Tyne & Wear

No natural forests were destroyed to make this product;
only farmed timber was used and replanted.

A CIP catalogue record for this book is available from the British Library.

Main Work	ISBN 0421 905 808
First Supplement	ISBN-10 0-421-95610-0
	ISBN-13 978-0-421-95610-0

HOW TO USE THIS SUPPLEMENT

This supplement follows the same order of material as the book: commentary on PACE; commentary on the relevant part of the Police Reform Act 2002 and the text of those sections of the 2002 Act; PACE; and the revised codes of practice.

At the end of the supplement there is a new appendix consisting of the Notice of Rights and Entitlements given to suspects in the police station.

After consulting the relevant part of the main work, reference should therefore be made to the equivalent section in the supplement to see if there is new material. Paragraph numbers quoted in the supplement refer to the same paragraph number in the main volume.

All references in the text to cases and statutes are contained in the tables printed at the beginning of this supplement.

INTRODUCTION

When the fifth edition of this book went for printing, the Serious Organised Crime and Police Bill had not yet reached the statute book. The fifth edition dealt with the changes to PACE and to the Police Reform Act 2002 made by the Bill as it stood on first publication in November 2004. The Bill eventually received Royal Assent and became an Act on April 7, 2005 (the abbreviation "SOCPA" is used throughout). There were numerous changes from the Bill to the Act—mostly in regard to clause and section numbers, though there were also some substantive changes. In April 2005 a 12-page memo on the publishers' website (*www.sweetandmaxwell.co.uk*) enabled readers to amend their copy of the book by inserting the necessary alterations.

In summer 2005 the Home Office circulated for consultation a revised version of the PACE Codes. The revised Codes were laid before Parliament on November 8. They were approved by the House of Commons on November 30 and by the House of Lords on December 9. The revised codes and their accompanying statutory provisions[1] came into force on January 1, 2006. The Home Office issued guidance to the police regarding the new Codes—Circular 56/2005. The revised Codes and the Home Office Circular are accessible on the Home Office PACE website: *http://police.homeoffice.gov.uk/operational-policing/powers-pace-codes/pace-codes.html*.

The main effect of the revision, which includes a new Code G on arrest, was to implement the provisions of SOCPA and the Drugs Act 2005.

This Supplement reflects the changes made by the statutory changes and by the revised codes. It also deals with new case law.

The Northern Ireland Office plans to introduce changes similar to those made in England and Wales. A draft PACE (Amendment) Northern Ireland Order 2006 and draft codes were due to be published for consultation in February 2006 with a view to implementation later in the year. The main focus of the Order would be changes to PACE similar to those in SOCPA plus amendments based on the Criminal Justice and Police Act 2001, the Police Reform Act 2002 and the Criminal Justice Act 2003. Changes to the PACE codes were to be modelled on those introduced as from January 1, 2006 in England and Wales.

The supplement is up-to-date to January 2006.

---

[1] See Police and Criminal Evidence Act 1984 (Codes of Practice) Order 2005, SI 2005/3503; Serious Organised Crime and Police Act 2005 (Commencement No.4 & Transitory Provisions) Order, SI 2005/3495; Serious Organised Crime and Police Act 2005 (Amendment) Order 2005, SI 2005/3496. See also Drugs Act 2005 (Commencement No.3) Order 2005, SI 2005/3053.

THE BACKGROUND AND THE FUTURE

The future for the Codes

p.xv. In introducing the 2006 revision of the Codes on December 9, 2005, the Home Office Minister, Lord Bassam, told the House of Lords (col.929):

> "Work will be starting in February next year to look how to improve the form and content of the codes. This will include the potential incorporation of statutory guidance which can be subject to amendment administratively to take faster, more effective account of best practice and lessons learnt."

So the Home Office did have plans for changes to the codes but at the time of writing the nature of such impending changes remained to be revealed. The Minister's statement can hardly be said to have been very informative.

CONTENTS

TABLE OF CASES

TABLE OF STATUTES

COMMENTARY ON THE ACT

POWERS TO STOP AND SEARCH

Definitions of powers to stop and search: s.1

PACE and Code A

Para.1–07, p.6, n.11. Change "cl.106" to "s.115(5)".

"Reasonable suspicion"

Religion as a basis for stop and search

Para.1–09, p.6. A person's religion cannot be considered as reasonable grounds for suspicion and must never be considered as reason to stop or to stop and search a person. (Code A, para.2.2, 2006 revision.)

Stop and search by Community Support Officers

New para.1–30A, p.18, at end. The 2006 revision of Code A includes a new Annex C (p.86 below) setting out the powers of Community Support Officers regarding stop, search and seizure. Part 1 lists the powers to stop and search not requiring consent of the person.[2] Part 2 sets out the powers to search requiring consent of the person searched.[3] Part 3 sets out the powers to search not

---

[1] See Police and Criminal Evidence Act 1984 (Codes of Practice) Order 2005, SI 2005/3503; Serious Organised Crime and Police Act 2005 (Commencement No.4 & Transitory Provisions) Order, SI 2005/3495; Serious Organised Crime and Police Act 2005 (Amendment) Order 2005, SI 2005/3496. See also Drugs Act 2005 (Commencement No.3) Order 2005, SI 2005/3053.

[2] Items intended to be used in connection with terrorism under Terrorism Act 2000, ss.44(1)(a),(d), (2)(b) and s.45(2).

[3] Alcohol or a container for alcohol—under Criminal Justice and Police Act 2001, s.12(2); alcohol— under Confiscation of Alcohol (Young Persons) Act 1997, s.1; tobacco or cigarette papers—under Children and Young Persons Act 1933, s.7(3).

requiring the consent of the person.[4] Part 4 sets out the power to seize without consent.[5]

Duty to make records concerning searches: s.3 and Code A, s.4

Electronic recording

Para.1–32, p.20. When an officer makes a record of the stop electronically and is unable to produce a copy of the form at the time, the officer must explain how the person can obtain a full copy of the record of the stop or search and give the person a receipt which contains: a unique reference number and guidance on how to obtain a full copy of the stop or search; the name of the officer who carried out the stop or search (unless the exception where giving the name would endanger the officer applies); and the power used to stop and search them. (Code A, para.4.10A, 2006 revision.)

A new duty to record stops not involving a search

Para.1–34, p.21. The 2006 revision of Code A adds to para.4.19 that the officer can refuse to issue the form "if he or she reasonably believes that the purpose of the request is deliberately aimed at frustrating or delaying legitimate police activity". Lord Bassam, the Home Office Minister, told the House of Lords on December 9, 2005 that the Government intended to remove the requirement to make a record where the criteria are not met and thereby "minimise the ability of those who may wish to deliberately waste an officer's time by asking for a record when an encounter has not taken place in accordance with Code A" (col.930).

For an empirical study of the new system see M. Shiner, *National implementation of the recording of police stops*, January 2006, Home Office website (*www.homeoffice.gov.uk*) published only online.

Road checks: s.4

Para.1–39, p.24, n.17. *R. (Gillan and Quinton) v Cmnr. of the Metropolitan Police* The case is now reported at [2004] EWCA Civ 1067, [2005] 1 All E.R.970 and at [2005] Crim.L.R. 414. See also the lengthy commentary in the *Criminal Law Review* at pp.416–418.

---

[4] Objects that might be used to cause physical injury or to assist escape—under PACE s.32.
[5] Controlled drugs—under Police Reform Act 2002, Sch.4, para.7B.

PART II

POWERS OF ENTRY, SEARCH AND SEIZURE

Applications to justices of the peace for search warrants: s.8

Para.2–06, p.44, line 2. SOCPA also made significant changes in regard to search warrants—see para.2–43 below.

Common law still applies to extradition crimes

Para.2–11, p.46, n.23. *Hewitson* is [2003] EWHC 3296 (Admin).

Access to "excluded" and "special procedure" material: s.9 and Sch.1

Paras.2–14 to 2–20, pp.48–52, Sch.1. In s.8 and in Sch.1 "serious arrestable offence" is replaced by "indictable offence" (SOCPA, Sch.7, para.43(3), (13)). See further para.2–43. (An indictable offence is one triable only on indictment or one that can be tried either in the magistrates' court or in the Crown Court.)

Search warrants

Para.2–19, p.51. A search warrant issued by the judge can be an "all premises warrant" as provided for in SOCPA, s.113(10) to (14).

Para.2–20, p.51. *R. (on the application of Energy Financing Team Ltd) v Bow Street Magistrates' Court* [2005] EWHC 1626 (Admin), [2005] 4 All E.R. 285 concerned search warrants issued where it is not practicable to serve a notice requiring a person to produce documents or where such a notice might seriously prejudice the investigation. The Divisional Court's wide-ranging decision gave guidance on both the principles and the practice: 1) It is always necessary to consider whether a less intrusive alternative way could be found to obtain the material. 2) The applicant must give the judge full assistance—including pointing out anything that militated against issue of the warrant. 3) The application should be made with sufficient specificity to permit those executing the warrant and those affected by it to tell whether a document or class of documents fell within its terms. 4) The judge should be given time to pre-read the application. 5) The decision should be briefly reasoned. 6) A record should be made of the decision. 7) Tape recording of the proceedings was best, failing which, if any issue had arisen, the applicant should prepare a note which should be submitted to the judge for approval. 8) The judge had no jurisdiction to reconsider his decision once the warrant had been executed. The remedy then was judicial review. 9) In deciding whether to grant permission for judicial review the court would bear in mind that the seizure of documents pursuant to a search warrant was an investigative step which was perhaps best considered at the trial. 10) Although it might not be appropriate fully to inform the person affected as to all the information disclosed to the judge, he should be given as much information as possible as to the material put before the judge and as to what happened at the hearing so as to enable him to take meaningful legal advice.

Safeguards for obtaining search warrants: ss.15 and 16 and PACE Code B, s.2

SOCPA provisions on search warrants and Schedule 1 applications

Para.2–43, p.66, line 2. The relevant provisions are to be found in ss.113 and 114 of SOCPA and in Code B, s.3.

Para.2–43, p.66

- end of first indented para.—change "cl.105(2)" to "s.114(2) and Code B, para.6.3A"

- first bullet point—change "cl.105(4) of the Bill" to "s.114(4) of the Act and Code B, para.3.6(db)"

- second bullet point—change "cl.105(6) of the Bill" to "s.114(6) of the Act"

Para.2–43, p.67

- first bullet point—change "cl.105(7) of the Bill" to "s.114(7) of the Act"

- second bullet point—change "cl.105(8)(a) of the Bill" to "s.114(8)(a) of the Act and Code B, para.6.1"

- third bullet point—change " cl.105(8)(b) of the Bill" to "s.114(8)(b) of the Act and Code B, para.6.3A"

- fourth bullet point—change "cl.105(8)(c) of the Bill" to "s.114(8)(c) of the Act and Code B, para.8.3"

- fifth bullet point—add at end, "(s.113(4))"

- sixth bullet point—add at end, "(s.113(4))"

- seventh bullet point—add at end, "(s.113(7) and Code B, para.3.6(da))". (NB It appears that due to a drafting oversight the new subs.(2A) only applies to applications made under s.8 of PACE and does not apply to applications made under other Acts such as the Theft Act—see Richard Stone, 'Impossible Conditions for search warrants', *New Law Journal*, November 11, 2005, p.1710.)

Para.2–43, p.68

- first bullet point—add at end, "(s.114(8))"

- second bullet point—add at end, "(s.114(9)(a) and Code B, para.6.3B)"

- third bullet point—add at end, "(s.114(9)(b) and Code B, para.8.2)"

- fourth bullet point—add at end, "(s.113(14))"

Note that search warrant powers arising from statutes other than PACE are not affected by the introduction of multiple entry and "all premises" warrants. They remain limited to single entry and single premises.

Execution of warrants: s.16 and Code B

Para.2–45, p.69. An officer of the rank of inspector or above may direct a designated investigating officer not to wear a uniform for the purposes of a specific operation. (SOCPA, s.122(2) amending s.42(2) of the Police Reform Act 2002; Code B, Note 2G). The Home Office Circular 56/2005 states: "Where a designated investigating officer is not in uniform the individual must carry proof of their designation as a measure of proving their identity and confirming the powers at their disposal."

Entry for purpose of arrest, etc.: s.17

Para.2–61, p.78, s.17(1)(b). SOCPA, Sch.7, Pt.3, para.43(4) substituted "indictable" for "arrestable". Note that the power to arrest for the summary offences listed in s.17(1)(c), (ca) and (caa) remain.

Para.2–61, p.78, s.17(1)(c). SOCPA, Sch.7, Pt.4, para.58 added:

- driving when under the influence of drink or drugs, under the Road Traffic Act 1988, s.4 (s.17(1)(c)(iiia))

- offences involving drink or drugs, under the Transport and Works Act 1992, s.27 (s.17(1)(c)(iiib)).

- offences under the Animal Health Act 1981, s.61 (s.17(1)(caa)).

Para.2–62, p.79 add at end. For a case in which entry was justified to make an arrest for breach of the peace see *Blench v DPP* [2004] EWHC 2717 (Admin), [2004] All E.R.(D) 86 (Nov).

Entry and search after arrest: s.18

Para.2–64, p.80. This whole paragraph must now be seen in light of the provisions of SOCPA which, as from January 1, 2006, restricts the s.18 power of entry and search of premises to situations where the arrest was for an indictable offence. (SOCPA, Sch.7, para.43(5) and Code B, para.4.3, 2006 revision).

What is the procedure for search warrants?

Para.2–97, p.98. Under SOCPA, as from January 1, 2006:

- a search warrant may authorise multiple entries;

- a search warrant can relate to named premises ("a specific premises warrant") or to any premises "occupied or controlled " by a named person (an "all premises warrant");

- a search warrant can be executed within three months (instead of one month as before).

PART III

ARREST

Arrest without warrant for arrestable and other offences: s.24

SOCPA changes to law of arrest and new Code G

Para.3–04, p.104 n.7, add at end. The changes made by SOCPA in regard to arrest powers do not apply (as yet) in Northern Ireland. The Criminal Justice (Northern Ireland) Order 2005, Art.23 amended Art.26 of the 1989 Northern Ireland PACE Order (list of offences to which powers of summary arrest apply), by adding five offences under the Sexual Offences Act 2003: exposure (s.66); voyeurism (s.67); intercourse with an animal (s.69); sexual penetration of a corpse (s.70); and sexual activity in a lavatory (s.71). The Prevention of Terrorism Act 2005, s.9(3) added the offence of obstructing the delivery of a control order under s.7(9) of the Act. The Firearms (Amendment) (Northern Ireland) Order 2005, Art.5(3) added the offence of carrying a firearm in a public place in respect of an air gun or an imitation firearm—contrary to Art.61(1) of the Firearms (Northern Ireland) Order 2004.

Para.3–04, p.104, end of first sub-para. As from January 1, 2006, SOCPA makes all offences arrestable, abolishes the category of "serious arrestable offences" (SAOs) and applies the additional powers previously available for SAOs to indictable offences. The 2006 revision of the Codes includes a new six-page Code G (p.120 below) dealing solely with arrest.

Code G opens with a statement of the need to use the power of arrest sparingly:

"1.2   The right to liberty is a key principle of the Human Rights Act 1998. The exercise of the power of arrest represents an obvious and significant interference with that right.

1.3   The use of the power must be fully justified and officers exercising the power should consider if the necessary objectives can be met by other, less intrusive means. Arrest must never be used simply because it can be used. Absence of justification for exercising the powers of arrest may lead to challenges should the case proceed to court. When the power of arrest is exercised it is essential that it is exercised in a non-discriminatory and proportionate manner."

Para.3–05, p.105, first para. Schedule 1A was repealed by SOCPA, Sch.7, para.24(3).

Para.3–05, p.105, second para. As from January 1, 2006, the extra powers previously available in respect of arrestable offences under ss.17, 18, 32 and 42 are in principle[6] only available for indictable offences. That means that most of the summary offences listed in PACE Sch.1A (now repealed) that previously had access to these "trigger powers" will no longer carry such powers. This has given rise to police concern. The Home Office Circular 56/2005 issued in December 2005 stated:

> "This was made known during both the consultation and legislative processes. However, we understand the concern about potential impact that may be caused with these changes. We are discussing with ACPO on an offence by offence basis the need for any further additions to section 17(1)(c)".

It is safe to predict that these discussions will result in the restoration of the "trigger powers" in respect of at least some of these offences.

(The Home Office Circular included a list of the summary offences which no longer attract trigger powers under ss.17(1)(b), 18(1), 32(2)(b) and 42(1)(b) of PACE:

- s.19 Firearms Act 1968—carrying firearm or imitation firearm in public place in respect of an air weapon or imitation firearm. Note that the Violent Crime Reduction Bill 2005–06 proposes that the offence becomes indictable.

- s.12 Theft Act 1968—taking motor vehicle or other conveyance without authority etc.;

- Wildlife and Countryside Act 1981 offences: s.1(1), (2) or 6—taking, possessing, selling etc. of wild birds specified in Sch.1 to that Act or any part of, or anything derived from, such a bird, s.1(5)—disturbance of wild birds, s.9 or 13(1)(a) or (2)—taking, possessing or selling etc. of wild animals or plants).

- s.39(1) Civil Aviation Act 1982—trespass on aerodromes.

- ss.21C(1) and 21D(1) Aviation Security Act 1982—unauthorised presence in a restricted zone or on an aircraft.

- s.1 Sexual Offences Act 1985—kerb-crawling.

- s.39 Criminal Justice Act 1988—Common Assault (declared an arrestable offence by s.10(1) Domestic Violence, Crime & Victims Act 2004)

---

[6] Section 17 entry to make an arrest still applies to the summary offences listed in s.17(1)(c)(i) to (iiib) and (caa).

- s.103(1)(b) Road Traffic Act 1988—driving while disqualified.

- s.170(4) Road Traffic Act 1988—failure to stop and report an accident in respect of an accident to which that section applies by virtue of s.170(1)(a) (accidents causing personal injury).

- s.14J or 21C of the Football Spectators Act 1989—(failing to comply with requirements imposed by or under a banning order or a notice under s.21B).

- All offences under the Football (Offences) Act 1991.

- s.60AA(7) Criminal Justice and Public Order Act 1994—failing to comply with requirement to remove disguise.

- s.66 Criminal Justice and Public Order Act 1994—sale of tickets by unauthorised persons.

- s.167 Criminal Justice and Public Order Act 1994—touting for car hire services.

- s.89(1) Police Act 1996—assaulting a police officer in the execution of his duty or a person assisting such an officer.

- s.2 of the Protection from Harassment Act 1997—harassment.

- s.12(4) Criminal Justice and Police Act 2001—failure to comply with requirements imposed by constable in relation to consumption of alcohol in public place.

- s.46 Criminal Justice and Police Act 2001—placing of advertisements in relation to prostitution.

- s.143(1) of the Licensing Act 2003—failure to leave licensed premises, etc.

- s.71 Sexual Offences Act 2003—sexual activity in public lavatory.

- s.9(3) Prevention of Terrorism Act 2005—obstructing entry/search under s.7(9) to deliver a control order notice.)

Para.3–05, pp.105–06, third para. Under the SOCPA changes, persons other than police officers can arrest only for indictable offences.

Para.3–13, p.111. It is enough that the arresting officer's suspicion relates to a category of offence—such as "VAT fraud". It does not have to be more specific (*Coudrat v Commissioners of Her Majesty's Revenue and Customs* [2005] EWCA Civ.616).

Information to be given on arrest: s.28

Para.3–22, p.116, line 1. Code C, para.10.3 in the 2006 revision refers the reader to Code C, para.3.4 and Code C, Note 10B and new Code G, paras.2.2 and 4.3.

Search upon arrest: s.32

Para.3–35, p.122, second para. Change first sentence to "Unlike the power to search under s.18, it was originally not limited to arrestable offences. However, the effect of SOCPA is that as from January 1, 2006, the s.32 power to search premises after an arrest only applies where the arrest was for an indictable offence (Sch.7, Part 3, para.43(6) and Code B, para.4.2, 2006 revision).

The Serious Organised Crime and Police Act 2005

Para.3–42, p.126, line 1. Change "Clause 101" to "Section 110".

Para.3–42, p.126, line 4. Code B, para.2.3 states, "A constable may arrest without warrant in relation to any offence except for the single exception listed in Note for Guidance 1". Note 1 refers to offences under Criminal Law Act 1967, s.4(1) (assisting offenders by impeding their arrest or prosecution) and s.5(1) (taking compensation for concealing offences). They only apply if the offences to which they relate carry a sentence fixed by law or are ones in which a first time offender aged 18 or over could be sentenced to five years or more.

The new necessity principle

Para.3–43, p.127, after (e) and (f). Code G places emphasis on the "necessity principle":

> "2.4 The power of arrest is *only* exercisable if the constable has reasonable grounds for believing that it is necessary to arrest the person. The criteria for what may constitute necessity are set out in paragraph 2.9."

Paragraph 2.9 spells out more fully the terms of what makes an arrest necessary. The terms of para.2.9 in regard to (a) to (d) are familiar. In regard to the two new criteria in s.110(5)—(e) and (f)—Code G says—

> "(e) to allow the prompt and effective investigation of the offence or of the conduct of the person in question.
>
> This may include cases such as:
>
> (i)   Where there are reasonable grounds to believe that the person:
>
> - has made false statements;

- has made statements which cannot be readily verified;
- has presented false evidence;
- may steal or destroy evidence;
- may make contact with co-suspects or conspirators;
- may intimidate or threaten or make contact with witnesses;
- where it is necessary to obtain evidence by questioning; or

(ii) When considering arrest in connection with an indictable offence, there is a need to:

- enter and search any premises occupied or controlled by a person;
- search the person;
- prevent contact with others;
- take fingerprints, footwear impressions, samples or photographs of the suspect.

(iii) Ensuring compliance with statutory drug testing requirements.

(f) to prevent any prosecution for the offence from being hindered by the disappearance of the person in question. This may arise if there are reasonable grounds for believing that:

- if the person is not arrested he or she will fail to attend court
- street bail after arrest would be insufficient to deter the suspect from trying to evade prosecution."

Information to be given to the arrested person

Section 3 of Code G sets out the requirements as regards the information that must be given to an arrested person and the cautions, taken from Code C, section 10. These include the reasons why an arrest is necessary (Code G, Note 3).

Records

Section 4 of Code G states that the officer must record—

- the nature and circumstances of the offence leading to the arrest

- the reason or reasons why arrest was necessary

- the giving of the caution

- anything said by the person at the time of arrest

Unless impracticable, the record must be made at the time of arrest (para.4.2). On arrival at the police station, the custody officer must open the custody record. The information given by the arresting officer as to the circumstances, etc. of the arrest must then be recorded as part of the custody record (or a copy of the record already made can be attached) (para.4.3).

Arrest not requiring the officer to be in uniform

The Home Office Circular on the changes being introduced as from January 1, 2006 states that the new power of arrest under s.24 does not require that the arresting officer be in uniform and that various statutory provisions[7] requiring that the officer be in uniform have been repealed.

Para.3–44, p.127, line 1. Change "cl.101" to "section 110".

Para.3–44, p.127, lines 4, 5 and 6. Insert the word "indictable" before the word "offence".

Para.3–45, p.128. This paragraph is no longer valid. The provision that was in cl.101(4) of the Bill is not in the Act. The common law power of arrest remains.

Repeal and retention of other statutory powers of arrest

Sch.2 of PACE lists 18 statutes with preserved arrest provisions. SOCPA, Sch.7, para.24(4) states that six of these are omitted from Sch.2. Those that remain include the power of arrest under s.7 of the Bail Act 1976 for absconding or breaking conditions of bail where the person is under a duty to surrender to a court, the arrest of military personnel and the arrest of persons under the Mental Health Act 1983 who are absent without leave or who have absconded.

Part 2 of Sch.7 of SOCPA lists eight miscellaneous further statutes with statutory powers of arrest that cease to have effect. They include arrest in connection with the power to disperse unlawful meetings under the Unlawful Drilling Act 1819 s.2, arrest for breach of bye-laws under the London County Council (General Powers) Act 1900 s.27, and arrest for taking or destroying fish under the Theft Act 1968 Sch.1, para.2(4).

---

[7] – Anti-social Behaviour Act 2003—ss.4(5), 32(3).
   – Criminal Justice and Police Act 2001—s. 42(8).
   – Criminal Justice and Public Order Act 1994—ss. 61(5), 63(8), 65(5), 68(4), 69(5), 76(7).
   – Public Order Act 1986—ss. 12(7), 13(10), 14(7), 14B(4), 14C(4).
   – Criminal Law Act 1977—ss 6(6), 7(6), 8(4), 9(7), 10(5).
   – Road Traffic Act 1988—s. 163(4).

QUESTIONS AND ANSWERS

ARREST

On what grounds can someone be arrested?

Para.3–54, p.131, last sentence. In the event, SOCPA did not abolish common law powers of arrest.

Part IV

DETENTION

Custody officers at police station: s.36

Delegation by custody officers to civilian support staff

Para.4–12, p.138, line 10. Change "Clauses 111 and 112" to "sections 120 and 121 and Code C, para.1.9, 2006 revision".

Duties of custody officer before charge: s.37

Para.4–13, p.138. *Retrial after an acquittal* When a person is arrested under the provisions of the Criminal Justice Act 2003 permitting the retrial of someone who has been acquitted of a serious offence, the detention provisions of PACE are modified in that the police decision as to whether there is sufficient evidence to charge must be made by an officer of the rank of superintendent who was not involved in the investigation (Code C, Note 16AA, 2006 revision).

Para.4–14, p.139, n.15. The following police areas were added on various dates in 2005 to those where the Director's Guidance applies: Cumbria, Durham, Gloucestershire, Hampshire, Hertfordshire, Lincolnshire, Norfolk, North Wales, North Yorkshire, South Wales, Suffolk, Sussex and West Mercia.

The force areas where the Guidance was not yet included as of January 2006 were: Bedfordshire, Cambridgeshire, Cheshire, Derbyshire, Dorset, Devon & Cornwall, Dyfed Powys, Essex, Gwent, Leicestershire, Northamptonshire, Staffordshire, Surrey, Warwickshire and Wiltshire.

Para.4–20, p.142, third para. Note 16AB was amended in the 2006 revision of the Codes—see para.4–33 below.

Detention time limits and new charging provisions

Paras.4–33—34, pp.149—50. The amended Note 16AB in the 2006 revision of
the Codes tries to meet the point. It no longer refers to an allowance of "reasonable time". Instead the Note states that the custody officer may detain the person
"for no longer than is reasonably necessary to decide how that person is to be
dealt with under PACE, section 37(7) (a) to (d), including where appropriate,
consultation with the Duty Prosecutor." It adds, "The period is subject to the maximum period of detention before charge determined by PACE, sections 41 to 44."
This is an improvement on the previous version of the Note but it does not resolve
the question whether statutory amendment is needed to legitimise detention of
someone for consultation with the Duty Prosecutor when it is plain that there is
enough evidence to charge.

Reviews of police detention: ss.40 and 40A

Para.4–45, p.157, second para, lines 2–4. For a list of categories technically not
covered by the statutory requirement of s.40 reviews who should nevertheless be
reviewed see Code C, Note 15B. The list includes persons detained at police stations on behalf of the Immigration Service. The 2006 revision of Code C added
to the list a person detained by order of a magistrates' court under the Criminal
Justice Act 1988, s.152, as amended by the Drugs Act 2005, to facilitate the
recovery of evidence after being charged with drug possession or drug trafficking
and suspected of having swallowed drugs (Note 15B(g)).

Authorisation of continued detection: s.42

Authorisation extended to all arrestable offences

Para.4–62, p.167, first sentence. As from January 1, 2006, this applies only to
indictable offences (SOCPA, Sch.7, para.43(7) and Code C, para.15.2A, 2006
revision).

Bail after arrest: s.47

No arrest for breach of conditions

Para.4–83, p.179, first para. Mr David Pickover (Legal Editor, *Police Review*,
24 December 5, 2004) suggested that the view expressed in this paragraph is mis-
taken. Section 1(1) of the Bail Act defines "bail in criminal proceedings' to
include, inter alia, bail grantable to a person in connection with an offence who
is under arrest. In his view, for the purposes of s.7(3) it makes no difference
whether the bail conditions are imposed by the court or by the police. This is

clearly correct if the person is bailed to appear at court. But the writer stands by his view that in regard to someone bailed to return to the police station there is no general power to arrest for actual or anticipated breach of bail conditions. Moreover, the exception created by the Criminal Justice Act 2003 referred to, applies only where there has been a breach of condition and does not apply to an anticipated breach.

Part V

QUESTIONING AND TREATMENT
OF PERSONS BY POLICE

Intimate searches and strip searches: s.55 and Code C, Annex A

Para.5–10, p.198, (4). Delete and substitute: "and the suspect must be informed of the giving of the authorisation and of the grounds for it (Drugs Act 2005, s.3(2) inserting new subs.(3B) in s.55)."

Insert new (5) "(5) if it is a drug offence search, the search requires the prior written consent of the suspect (Drugs Act 2005, s.3(2) inserting new subs.(3A) in s.55; Code C, Annex A, para.2(a)). The custody record must state the authorisation, the grounds for giving it and that consent was given (Drugs Act 2005, s.3(3) inserting new subs.(10A) in s.55)." (Note A6 to Annex A suggests the following words: "You do not have to allow yourself to be searched, but I must warn you that if you refuse without good cause, your refusal may harm your case if it comes to trial." This warning may be given by a police officer or a civilian staff member. A detainee who is not legally represented must be reminded of his entitlement to have free legal advice (Code C, Annex A, para.2B))."

Para.5–12, p.199, three sentences from end. The 2006 revision of Code C added the requirement that the custody record show that authorisation for the intimate search was given, the grounds and also the grounds for believing that the article could not be removed without such a search. In the case of a drugs offence intimate search, the record must also show that the required warning about the effect of refusal of consent was given and whether consent was given or refused—with the reason for refusal (Code C, Annex 2 para.7).

Para.5–15, p.201, at the end. Both proposals were adopted and are now to be found in the Serious Organised Crime and Police Act 2005. Section 8 of SOCPA gives magistrates the same power to remand a suspect to police detention for 192 hours as they already had in respect of customs detention under s.152 of the Criminal Justice Act 1988. Section 3(5) of the Drugs Act, allows for adverse inferences to be drawn from the refusal to permit a drug offence intimate search without reasonable cause (inserting a new subs. (13A) in s.55 of PACE).

X-rays and ultra sound scans: s.55A

New para.5–17A, p.202. The Drugs Act 2005, s.5 inserted into PACE a new s.55A called 'X-rays and ultrasound scans'. (The equivalent provisions for Northern Ireland are in s.6.)) The subject is dealt with in the Codes in a new Annex K to Code C. For the full texts of the section see pp.64 and 66 below.

The main features of the new power are:

- If an officer of inspector or higher rank has reasonable grounds for believing that someone in police detention after being arrested for an offence may have swallowed a Class A drug of which he was in possession before his arrest with the appropriate criminal intent,[8] he can authorise an x-ray or ultrasound scan (subs.(1)).

- The suspect must have consented in writing (subs.(2)). Adverse inferences can be drawn at a trial from refusal to give consent (subs.(9)).

- Before consent is sought, the suspect must be warned that refusal could lead to adverse inferences being drawn at a trial. An unrepresented suspect must be reminded of the entitlement to free legal advice (Code C, Annex K, para.3).

- In the case of a juvenile, an appropriate adult should be present when consent is sought (Code C, Annex K, para.6).

- The suspect must be informed that it has been authorised and why (subs.(3)).

- It must be done at a hospital or at a registered medical practitioner's surgery or other place used for medical purposes (subs.(4)).

- The custody record must as soon as practicable state the authorisation, its grounds, the warning required by para.3 of Code C, Annex K, and the fact that consent was given or refused. If an x-ray or scan is done, the record must show where, who carried it out, who was present and the result (subss.(5), (6), Code C, Annex K, para.5).

- Annual reports by the chief officer must give details including the number and results of such x-rays and ultrasound scans (subss.(7), (8)).

---

[8] As defined in s.55.

The right to have someone informed when arrested: s.56 and Code C, s.5 and Annex B

SAOs into indictable offences

Paras.5–19 and 5–20, p.203. Under SOCPA and the 2006 revision of the Codes, all references to serious arrestable offences become references to indictable offences.

Denial of or delay in giving suspect his rights

New para.5.7A of Code C states that any delay or denial of the rights in s.5 ('Right not to be held incommunicado') should be 'proportionate and should last no longer than necessary'.

The permitted telephone call

Para.5–25, p.205, first sentence. The 2006 revision of Code C, para.5.6 provides that the right to have writing materials or to make a telephone call can only be denied or delayed if the person has been arrested for an indictable offence.

   As noted above, new para.5.7A states that any delay or denial of the rights in s.5 ('Right not to be held incommunicado') should be 'proportionate and should last no longer than necessary'.

The right to legal advice: s.58

CDS Direct

Para.5–44, pp.215–16. In October 2005 the Legal Services Commission began a six-month pilot of a new method of delivering police station duty solicitor services through CDS Direct. (Originally it was intended that this commence in May 2005.) The main part of the pilot takes place in the area of the Liverpool and the Boston duty solicitor schemes. In those two areas requests for a duty solicitor go to CDS Direct unless it is an indictable-only offence or the case is one where the time of the interview with the suspect is known. The CDS lawyer gives initial advice and decides whether attendance by a solicitor is needed. If so, the case is referred to a solicitor providing criminal defence services. In addition, where the service is restricted to telephone-only advice all duty solicitor services throughout the country is handled by CDS Direct (*Legal Action,* April 2005, p.16, October 2005 p.12).

Delaying access to legal advice

Grounds for delay: s.58(8); Code C, s.6 and Annex B

Para.5–52, p.220, n.8a. For "para.(10)", substitute "para.43(10)".

Para.5–53, p.220–21, second and third sentences. The 2006 revision of Code C, Annex B, paras.2 and 9 replaced the previous text of those provisions. Delay is now permissible where there are reasonable grounds to believe that a person detained for an indictable offence has benefited from his criminal conduct (by reference to Part 2 of the Proceeds of Crime Act 2002) and the recovery of the value of the property constituting that benefit will be hindered by the exercise of either right.

Tape recording of interviews: s.60

Audio recording

Para.5–81, p.233. The 2006 revision of Code E changes all references to "tape" to "recording" and adds a new definition of "recording media" as "any removable, physical audio recording medium (such as magnetic tape, optical disc or solid state memory) which can be played and copied" (Code E, para.1.6 (aa)). Appropriate changes are made throughout to reflect this wider definition.

Video recording of interviews: s.60A

Para.5–97, p.240. Code F was slightly revised in 2005 and a new transitional version became effective as from November 1.

Para.5–99, p.241. The 2006 revision of Code F, para.4.8 adds that when any objections have been visually recorded or the suspect has refused to have his objections recorded, the interviewer shall say that the recording equipment is being turned off, giving the reason—unless he reasonably considers that the interview can continue with the visual recording still on. New Guidance Note 4G states that the interviewer should be aware that a decision to continue recording against the wishes of the suspect may be the subject of comment in court. If a separate audio recording is being made, the same applies. The officer should ask the person to record the reasons for refusing to agree to visual recording of the interview. If the person objects to audio recording of the interview, para.4.8 of Code E applies. This provides that after the person's objections have been recorded or the suspect has refused to have his objections recorded, the interviewer should turn off the recorder unless he reasonably considers that the interview can continue with the tape still on.

Impressions of footwear: s.61A

Para.5–106, p.244, line 5. Change "cl.109(2)" to "s.118(2)".

Para.5–106, p.244, n.14. change "cl.108(2) and (4) of the Bill" to "s.117(2) and (4) of the Act".

Para.5–106, p.244, n.15. change "cl.108(5) of the Bill" to "s.117(5) of the Act".

Para.5–106, p.244, n.16. change "cl.108(7) of the Bill" to "s.117(8) of the Act".

Para.5–106, pp.244–45. The 2006 revision of Code D includes a new s.4(C) dealing with the taking of footwear impressions. If the statutory conditions are satisfied, such impressions can be taken without consent from a suspect over the age of ten and, if necessary, reasonable force can be used to do so. Before any footwear impression is taken with, or without, consent the person must be informed of the reason for it to be taken, that in some circumstances the impression may be retained (see Annex F, Part (a)), but that if they are to be destroyed the person has the right to witness the process. A full record must be made (Code D, paras.4.16–4.21).

Intimate samples: s.62 and Identification Code D, s.17

Para.5–109, p.246, n.22. Change "cl.110 of the Bill" to "s.119 of the Act. See also Code D para.6.1(a)".

Fingerprints and samples: miscellaneous supplementary provisions: s.63A

Para.5–120, p.251, n.69. Change "cl.108(5) of the Bill" to "s.117(5) of the Act; and Code D, para.6.1(a)."

Taking a non intimate sample for a drug test: ss.63B and 63C

Paras.5–121—23, pp.252—53. The drug testing scheme has been further changed by the Drugs Act 2005, as a result of which s.17 of Code C has been considerably revised. (For the relevant provisions of the Drugs Act see pp.69–76 below. Home Office Circular 49/2005 issued guidance regarding the new drug testing.[9])

---

[9] The guidance is available at *www.drugs.gov.uk/publications-search/dip/guidance-drugsact2005? view=Standard&pubID=240213.*

The chief features of the changes made by the Drugs Act[10] are:

- It applies to those over 18 who have been arrested. Previously they had to have been charged. However, this remains a requirement for those between 14 and 18 (s.7(5) inserting new subs.(3) into PACE s.63B[11]).

- Where someone over 18 who has been arrested for a trigger offence would be entitled to be released from custody before a sample has been taken, it can still be taken if he is also under arrest for a non-trigger offence providing that it is taken within 24 hours (s.7(9) inserting new subs.(5C) into s.63B).

- A person suspected of possession of a controlled drug or of drug trafficking can be remanded by magistrates to police detention for up to 192 hours (s.8 amending s.152 of the Criminal Justice Act 1988).

- If as a result of drug testing it is found that a specified Class A drug may be present, he can, before release, be required to attend an initial assessment and to remain for its duration (Drugs Act, s.9(2)). The person must be told when and where it will take place, that that will be confirmed to him in writing and that he may be liable to prosecution for failure to attend (s.11(2), (3)). At the same as he imposes a requirement to attend an initial assessment, the officer must require the person to attend a follow-up assessment unless he is informed at the initial assessment that this is not necessary (s.10(2)). He must be told that he may be liable to prosecution for failure to attend (s.11(4)).

- He must be given a written notice setting out the requirements and repeating the warnings (s.11(5)).

- A full record must be made in the custody record regarding what has been done—regarding a requirement under ss.9(2) and 10(2), information given under s.11(2), warnings given under ss.11(3) and (4), and notice given under s.11(5) (s.11(7)).

- An initial assessment is an appointment with a suitably qualified person for the purpose of establishing whether the person "is dependent

---

[10] For the most recent commencement order see Drugs Act 2005 (Commencement No.3) Order 2005, SI 2005/3053. This brought into effect as from December 1, 2005 the provisions relating to testing for Class A drugs and relating to the power to require a person to attend an initial assessment. It brought into effect as from January 1, 2006 the provisions in Part 1 of the Act relating, inter alia, to drug offence searches (s.3), x-rays and ultrasound scans (s.5) and extended detention of suspected drug offenders (s.8).

[11] Section 7 came into effect on December 1, 2005 under SI 2005/3053. Drug testing for under-eighteens was brought into force as from the same date by the Criminal Justice Act 2003 (Commencement No.11) Order 2005—SI 2005/No.3055. The power to test for drugs and to require an initial assessment only applies however where the chief officer has been notified by the Secretary of State that the necessary facilities are in place.

upon or has a propensity to misuse any specified Class A drug", and if so, whether he would benefit from further assessment or from assistance or treatment (or both) (s.9(3)).

- At a follow-up assessment, the assessor may draw up a care plan for further assistance or treatment (or both) (s.10(3),(4)).

- The offence of not attending an initial assessment or a follow-up assessment carries a maximum prison sentence of 51 weeks or a fine up to level 4 (s.12(4), s.14(4)).

- Information obtained as a result of an initial assessment or a follow-up assessment may not without the person's consent be disclosed to anyone save for the purposes of such assessments (s.15).

Drug testing for under-eighteens was brought into force as from December 1, 2005 by Criminal Justice Act 2003 (Commencement No.11) Order 2005, SI 2055/3055.

The drug testing provisions only apply in areas and police stations specified by the Secretary of State as having the necessary facilities. The 2006 revision drops Annex I and Annex J of Code C. (Note 72 on p.252 of the main work is therefore amended.)

The redrafted s.17 of Code C (see pp.97–102 below), which includes renumbering, incorporates all the above provisions. The catalogue of trigger offences now includes handling stolen goods, and begging. It also includes attempts to commit theft, robbery, burglary, obtaining property by deception and handling.

Photographing of subjects: s.64A and Identification Code D, s.5

Para.5–125, p.254, n.81. Change "cl.107(2) of the Bill" to "s.116 of the Act". Code D, para.3.30 in the 2006 revision removes the words "detained at police stations"—thereby applying the paragraph to photographs taken anywhere. See also revised Code D, para.5.12.

Para.5–125, p.254, n.86. Change "cl.107(3) of the Bill" to "s.116(5) of the Act".

Para.5–125, p.254, nn.88 and 89. Insert at start "Anti-Terrorism, Crime and Security Act 2001," and at end "See also revised Code D, new para.5.12A(b)."

Para.5–125, p.254. Insert at end "This broader definition means that moving images can now be retained in the same way as still photos."

Para.5–126, p.254, first para. Add at end "The power to take photographs elsewhere than at a police station is extended to community support officers and accredited persons. (SOCPA, Sch.8, paras.12 and 21.)"

Para.5–126, p.254 end of second para. Code D, new Note 5F states that:

"The use of reasonable force to take the photograph of a suspect elsewhere than at a police station must be carefully considered. In order to obtain a suspect's consent and co-operation to remove an item of religious headwear to take their photograph, a constable should consider whether in the circumstances of the situation the removal of the headwear and the taking of the photograph should be by an officer of the same sex as the person. It would be appropriate for these actions to be conducted out of public view."

Destruction of fingerprints, samples and photographs: s.64/Criminal Justice and Police Act 2001, s.82 and Code D, Annex F

Samples need no longer be destroyed

Para.5–132, p.257. Footwear impressions are subject to the same rules as fingerprints and samples. (See Code D, Annex F as amended in the 2006 revised version.)

Para.5–134, p.258, n.13. Change "cl.108(7) of the Bill" to "s.117(8) of the Act".

Para.5–134, p.258. Insert at end "Photographs taken in connection with identification procedures (under Code D, paras.3.5–3.10, para.3.21 or 3.23) which are taken other than under the provisions of Code D, para.5.12 must be destroyed unless the person has been charged, cautioned or prosecuted for a recordable offence or he has given informed written consent to their retention (Code D, para.3.31). (An example would be a photograph of someone who comes to the police station voluntarily. Para.5.12 would not apply as he would not have been detained at the police station.)

Photographs taken of identifying marks may be retained (PACE s.54A(9)(b) and Code D para.5.1). Photographs taken of persons detained at a police station or detained elsewhere in accordance with Code D, para.5.12 can equally be retained (PACE s.64A(4)(b) and Code D, para.5.12A(b))."

Definitions relating to fingerprints and samples: s.65

Para.5–136, p.259, line 4. Change "cl.110" to "s.119".

QUESTIONS AND ANSWERS

THE EXERCISE OF POLICE POWERS IN THE POLICE STATION

Can a suspect in the police station be photographed?

Para.5–160, p.273. Under SOCPA, photographs can now be taken elsewhere than at a police station—see para.5–125.

PART VI

THE CODES OF PRACTICE

Codes of practice: ss.66–67 and the Codes

Application of Codes to investigations elsewhere

Paras.6–15 to 6–17, pp.284–85. The Codes do not apply to criminal investigations abroad—*Fernandes, Fernandes and Travasso v The Governor of HM Prison Brixton and the Commonwealth of the Bahamas* [2004] EWHC 2207 (Admin), an extradition case. Note however that Extradition Act 2003, Codes of Practice B, C and D were brought into effect as from January 2004 (Extradition Act 2003 (Police Powers: Codes of Practice) Order 2003 SI No.3336).

Conditions of detention: Code C, s.8

Visiting the detainee

Para.6–33, p.293, end of first full para. The 2006 revision of Code C adds that visits prescribed by para.9.3 of Code C apply also to a person in custody by order of a magistrates' court under the Criminal Justice Act 1988, s.152 as amended by the Drugs Act 2005, s.8 to facilitate the recovery of evidence after being charged with drug possession or drug trafficking who is suspected of having swallowed drugs. In the case of the healthcare needs of a person who has swallowed drugs, the custody officer, subject to any clinical directions, should consider the necessity for rousing the suspect every half hour—though this does not negate the need for regular visiting of the suspect in his cell (New Note 9CA).

Medical treatment: Code C, s.9

Para.6–35, p.294, first sentence. The 2006 revision of Code C added the words "medically prescribed" before the words "controlled drugs". It also deleted the reference to Sch.1 in the second sentence.

"The appropriate adult"

Para.6–62, p.310, n.71. The 2006 revision of Code C, Note 1E states, "An appropriate adult is not subject to legal privilege."

Charging of persons in custody: s.16

Further questioning

Para.6–76, p.316, second para. For a case in which it was held that further questioning was not permitted because there was no ambiguity in the no-comment interview which required clearing up see *F v CPS and Chief Constable of Merseyside Police* [2003] EWHC 3266 (Admin)[12].

Code D: Identification

Para.6–78, p.317, first para., n.94. Add *Lambert and Foley* [2004] EWCA 154, [2004] All E.R. (D)01 (Sep); and *Lydiate* [2004] EWCA] 245.

Para.6–79, p.318, at the end. The 2006 revision of Code D dealt primarily with provisions regarding footwear impressions flowing from SOCPA s.118—see para.5–106.

Para.6–89, p.322, first para. After a video parade is ruled out there is nothing that requires that the next thing to consider is an identification parade—*Stott*[13].

Which procedure?

Para.6–89, p.322, second para., line 2. As to unusual features, see the new provision in Code D, Annex A, para.2A, dealt with below in para.6–100.

Vulnerable suspects and witnesses

Para.6–92, p.323. The 2006 revision of Code D has slightly different provisions for suspects and witnesses. Para.2.15 now deals only with suspects who are mentally disordered, otherwise mentally vulnerable suspects or juveniles who must have an appropriate adult present if they participate in any identification procedure. New para.2.15A states that any identification procedure involving a witness who is, or who appears to be, mentally disordered, otherwise mentally vulnerable or a juvenile should take place in the presence of a pre-trial support person. The support person must not be allowed to prompt identification of a suspect by

---

[12] (2003) 168 J.P. 93.
[13] [2004] EWCA Crim 615, [2004] All E.R. (D) 520.

the witness. New Note 2AB states that the Youth Justice and Criminal Evidence Act 1999 guidance "Achieving Best Evidence in Criminal Proceedings" indicates that a pre-trial support person should accompany a vulnerable witness during any identification procedure. It states that this support person should not be (or not be likely to be) a witness in the investigation.

Video identification (Code D, Annex A)

Para.6–100, pp.326–27. The 2006 revision of Code D, para.3.5, states that moving images must be used unless either the suspect is known but is not available (see para.3.21) or in accordance with para.2A of Annex A of Code D, the IO does not consider that replication of a distinctive physical feature can be achieved or that it is not possible to conceal the feature on the image of the suspect. In either case the IO may then decide to make use of still images.

Unusual physical features

Para.6–100, p.326. The 2006 revision of Code D inserted a new paragraph regarding a suspect who has unusual physical features, such as a facial scar, tattoo or distinctive hairstyle or hair colour. Steps may be taken in such a case to conceal the location of the feature on the image of the suspect or to replicate the feature on the images of the other people—electronically or by any other practicable method. If the witness has described an unusual physical feature, it should if possible be replicated. If it has not been described, concealment may be more appropriate (Code D, Annex A, para.2A). Either way, the decision and the reason for the decision should be recorded (Annex A, para.2B). If, where an unusual feature has been concealed or replicated, the witness asks to see an image without that feature, he may be allowed to do so (Annex A, para.2C).

In *Marcus* [2004] EWCA Crim 3387 the police assembled a set of images of eight as the best available with the appellant's distinguishing features (grey hair and grey beard) masked. They also showed the witnesses a second video compilation of the same eight persons unmasked. The defence were only notified of the second series of images shortly before the identification procedure. The police officer in charge told the trial court that on the second compilation the appellant would "blatantly stand out" and that the procedure was "blatantly unfair" to the appellant. Despite this, the trial judge admitted the identification evidence. The Court of Appeal quashed the conviction. (For discussion see C. Taylor, "Video identification under PACE Code D: *R. v Marcus*", 9 *International Journal of Evidence and Proof*, 2005, pp.204–10.)

PART VII

EVIDENCE IN CRIMINAL PROCEEDINGS—GENERAL

Admissibility of co-accused's out-of-court confession: s.74

Para.8–07, p.341, at end. In *Hayter* [2005] UKHL 6 a 3-2 majority in the House of Lords used the policy of s.74 to create a new exception to the hearsay evidence rule. H, R and B were each convicted of murder after a joint trial. In order to prove H's guilt the prosecution first had to establish that R was the actual killer. The only proof of this was R's out-of-court admission to his girl-friend in which he implicated H as his recruiter and paymaster. The trial judge directed the jury to consider first the case of R, then of B and H. An out-of-court confession is generally evidence only against its maker. Upholding H's conviction, the majority (Lords Bingham, Steyn and Brown) used the policy of s.74 to create a new exception to the hearsay evidence rule by allowing that a finding of guilt of one accused in a joint trial could be used by the jury as a building-block leading to the conviction of another of the defendants. The two dissenters (Lords Rodger and Carswell), considered that it was for Parliament rather than the courts to create new exceptions to the hearsay rule. (For critical commentary see D.M. Dwyer, "The Admissibility of a Confession agaist a Co-defendant: *R. v Hayter*", (2005) 68 *Modern L.R.* 839–48; [2005] Crim.L.R. 721–22. See also Professor D. Birch's commentary on the Court of Appeal's decision in [2003] Crim. L.R. 887–88.)

Section 76(1)

Para.8–13, p.343. Section 76 does not apply to disciplinary proceedings in a school—*R. v Independent Appeal Panel* [2004] EWHC 1831 (Admin). It was argued unsuccessfully that a statement made by a pupil admitting the offence should have been excluded under s.76 at a hearing of the Panel resulting in his permanent exclusion on a drugs charge.

Section 76(2)

Para.8–16, p.345, after first para. It is for the judge to rule on the admissibility of the confession and for the jury to consider its weight. However, if the judge admits a confession after a voir dire in which the defence challenged the confession on the ground that it was obtained as a result of oppression, he must direct the jury that they may not accept the confession if they believe that it was or may have been obtained in such a way. It is not open to him to direct the jury that they may rely on the confession if they think that, notwithstanding the way it may have been obtained, it was true. This was the opinion, technically obiter, of Lords Rodger, Phillips, Steyn and Carswell (Lord Hutton dissenting) in *Mushtaq* [2005] UKHL 25 overturning the view of the Court of Appeal. The four in the majority based their decision on the requirements of a fair trial enshrined in Art.6(1) of the European Convention on Human Rights. Their views were obiter as the law lords all agreed that since on the facts there was no actual evidence of oppression, the issue did not arise.

What is a confession?

Para.8–18, pp.345–46. Correction—The effect of the decision in *Z* was incorrectly stated by the writer. The Court of Appeal held that the question whether a statement was a confession had to be judged at the time of trial not, as determined in *Sat-Bhambra*, at the time it was made. However, on appeal, the House of Lords held that the Court of Appeal was wrong—the question should be decided at the time the statement was made. The House of Lords appeal is reported as *Hasan* [2005] UKHL 22. It follows that a statement that when made is exculpatory or neutral cannot be excluded under s.76 even though by the time the case reaches trial it is adverse to the accused.

Exclusion of "unfair evidence": s.78

Breaches of PACE and/or the Codes not condoned

Para.8–65. p.369. D not cautioned—Add *Mullings*[14]; *Armas-Rodriguez*[15].

Breaches of PACE and/or the Codes condoned

Para.8–66, p.372. No caution where one is required—Add *Senior and Senior*[16].

Para.8–66, p.372. Search warrant not shown—Add *Thomas*[17].

---

[14] [2004] EWCA Crim 2875, [2004] All E.R.134 (Nov).
[15] [2005] EWCA Crim 1081.
[16] [2004] EWCA Crim 454, [2004] 2 Cr.App.R. 215, [2004] 3 All E.R. 9, [2004] Crim.L.R. 749.
[17] [2004] EWCA Crim 590.

Para.8–66, p.373. Identification evidence allowed in despite breach of PACE or Code—Add *Royes*[18], *Toth*[19].

Para.8–68, p.375. Evidence obtained by undercover work held admissible—*Allsop and others*[20]; *Briggs-Price*[21].

Para.8–68, p.376. For a case following *Looseley* see *Moon*[22].

---

[18] [2004] EWCA Crim 3470.
[19] [2005] EWCA Crim 754.
[20] [2005] EWCA Crim 703.
[21] [2005] EWCA Crim 368.
[22] [2004] EWCA Crim 2872, [2004] All E.R.(D) 167 (Nov.).

PART XI

MISCELLANEOUS AND SUPPLEMENTARY

Application of Act to Armed Forces: s.113

Para.11–03, p.398, second para. For "serious arrestable offence" now read "indictable offence" (Serious Organised Crime and Police Act 2005 (Powers of Arrest) (Consequential Amendments) Order—SI 2005/ No.3389, para.12).

Application of Act to Customs and Excise: s.114

Paras.11–05—06, p.399. The Commissioners for Revenue and Customs Act 2005 amalgamated the prosecution forces of the Inland Revenue and Customs and Excise under the new organisation called the Revenue and Customs Prosecutions Office (RCPO) as part of the new department called HM Revenue and Customs. Sections 6 and 7 and Sch.1 of the Act transferred the powers of the existing staffs to the new organisation but powers previously exercised by Customs and Excise staff cannot be exercised in respect of matters inherited from Inland Revenue and *vice versa* (see Sch.2, para.7[23]).

Para.11–06, p.399, second para. For "arrestable offence" now read "indictable offence" (Serious Organised Crime and Police Act 2005 (Powers of Arrest) (Consequential Amendments) Order—SI 2005/ No.3389, para.2(2)).

Abolition of "serious arrestable offence": s.116

Para.11–09, p.401, line 4. After "Pt 3", insert "para.43(10)".

[23] For the Northern Ireland equivalent see para.9.

POLICE POWERS FOR CIVILIANS

CHAPTER 12

THE POLICE REFORM ACT 2002

Unless otherwise indicated, the italicised passages in the Fifth Edition showing the text of provisions of the Serious Organised Crime and Police Bill are confirmed and should be read as references to the Serious Organised Crime and Police Act 2005 (abbreviated "SOCPA"). The changes indicated mainly flow from a difference in the numbering and some additional material.

Police powers for police authority employees: s.38

Para.12–07, p.413, line 3. The details of the changes are helpfully set out in the Explanatory Notes to the Act, pp.54–62.

Community support officers: Sch.4, Pt 1

A power to detain for 30 minutes

Para.12–10, p.414, n.25. Change "of the Bill" to "of the Act".

Para.12–10, p.414, n.26. Change "para.3" to "para.4".

Other powers

Para.12–11, p.415, n.27. Delete and substitute: "Sch.8, paras 4, 6, 8, 9, 10, 11, 12, 16."

Investigating officers: Sch.4, Pt 2

Para.12–12, p.415, first bullet point. SOCPA[24] extends the powers of designated investigating officers in relation to the application for, and execution of search warrants in line with the new types of warrants than can be applied for.

---

[24] Sch.8, paras.13–15.

Thus para.16(a) of Sch.4 allows them to apply for any kind of warrant under s.8 of PACE in relation to any premises regardless of whether they are in the relevant police area ie the force area of the chief officer responsible for their designation. Para.17(b)(ii) allows a designated investigating officer to apply under Sch.1 for an "all premises" warrant regardless of whether the premises is in the relevant police area. But an application by such a designated person under Sch.1 for a "specific premises" warrant can only be made in respect of premises within the relevant police area. Paragraphs 16(e) and 17 (bc) state that the same applies to the execution of search warrants. Paragraphs 16A and 16B enable them to apply for and to execute warrants to search premises in the relevant police area under the Theft Act 1968, s.26 and the Misuse of Drugs Act 1971, s.23(3).

Para.12–12, p.415, third bullet point. SOCPA, Sch.9, para.6 places a general duty on investigating officers to assist any officer or other designated person to keep control of a detainee or prevent him from escaping regardless of whether the individual is under their control at the time and enables him to use reasonable force. The power can only be exercised in the police station.

Detention officers: Sch.4, Pt 3

Para.12–13, p.416. SOCPA, Sch.9, para.7 extends the same duty and powers regarding keeping the suspect under control as apply to investigating officers (para.12–12 above) to detention officers.

Escort officers: Sch.4, Pt 4

Para.12–14, p.416, first bullet point. SOCPA, Sch.9, para.8 states that escort officers have legal custody of a suspect under their control until the individual has been transferred into the custody of a police officer and places a duty on them to keep the individual under their control. The escort officer's duty to keep control of a detainee and to prevent them from escaping applies when they are at or in the vicinity of a police station.

Supplementary provisions relating to designations and accreditations: s.42

Para.12–19, p.419, n.31. Change "cl.113(2) of the Bill" to "s.122 of the Act".

POLICE REFORM ACT 2002

POLICE REFORM ACT 2002

All references to the Serious Organised Crime and Police Bill 2004–05 should be read as references to the 2005 Act.

PART 4

POLICE POWER ETC.

CHAPTER 1

EXERCISE OF POLICE POWERS ETC. BY CIVILIANS

Police powers for police authority employees: s.38

p.423, italicised passage, line 1. Change "cl.111(2)" to "s.120(2)".

p.423, n.1. Change "para.182(2)" to "para.181(2)" and in n.2 change "para.182(3)" to "para.181(3)".

p.424, first italicised passage, line 1. Change "cl.111(3)" to "s.120(3)".

p.424, second italicised passage, line 1. Change "cl.111(4)" to "s.120(4)".

p.424, n.3. Change "para.182(4)" to "para.181(4)".

Supplementary provisions relating to designations and accreditations: s.42

p.428, n.4. Change "cl.113(2)(a)" to "s.122(2)(a)".

p.429, first line. Change "cl.113(2)(b)" to "s.122(2)(b)".

p.429, n.5 and 6. Change "para.183" to "para.182".

Code of practice relating to chief officers' powers under Chapter 1: s.45

p.431, n.7. Change "para.184(2)" to "para.183(2)".

p.431, n.8. Change "para.184(3)" to "para.183(3)".

p.432, n.9. Change "para.184(4)" to "para.183(4)".

Interpretation of Chapter 1: s.47

p.433, nn.10 and 11. Change "para.185" to "para.184".

SCHEDULE 4

POWERS EXERCISABLE BY POLICE CIVILIANS

PART 1

COMMUNITY SUPPORT OFFICERS

Powers to issue fixed penalty notices: para.1

p.434, italicised passage after (d), line 1. Change "cl.113(3)(a)" to "s.122(3)(a)".

p.434, bottom of the page, after para.1. SOCPA, Sch.8, para.2 inserted new para.1A with seven sub-sections—

"Power to require name and address

1A—(1) This paragraph applies if a designation applies it to any person.

    (2) Such a designation may specify that, in relation to that person, the application of sub-paragraph (3) is confined to one or more only (and not to all) relevant offences or relevant licensing offences, being in each case specified in the designation.

    (3) Subject to sub-paragraph (4), where that person has reason to believe that another person has committed a relevant offence in the relevant police area, or a relevant licensing offence (whether or not in the relevant police area), he may require that other person to give him his name and address.

    (4) The power to impose a requirement under sub-paragraph (3) in relation to an offence under a relevant byelaw is exercisable only in a place to which the byelaw relates.

    (5) A person who fails to comply with a requirement under subparagraph (3) is guilty of an offence and shall be liable, on summary conviction, to a fine not exceeding level 3 on the standard scale.

    (6) In its application to an offence which is an offence by reference to which a notice may be given to a person in exercise of the power mentioned in paragraph 1(2)(aa), sub-paragraph (3) of this paragraph shall have effect as if for the words "has committed a relevant offence in the relevant police area" there were substituted "in the relevant police area has committed a relevant offence".

    (7) In this paragraph, "relevant offence", "relevant licensing offence" and "relevant byelaw" have the meaning given in paragraph 2 (reading accordingly the references to "this paragraph" in paragraph 2(6))."

Power to detain etc.: para.2

p.435, n.15. Delete the footnote since that addition to sub-para.(1) is not in the Act.

p.435, sub-para.2(2). SOCPA, Sch.8, para.3(2) substituted a new sub-para.2(2): "(2) A designation may not apply this paragraph to any person unless a designation also applies paragraph 1A to him."
So, n.16 no longer applies.

p.435. in sub-para.2(3), line 1. SOCPA, Sch.8, para.3(3)(a) substituted "paragraph 1A(3)" for "sub-paragraph (2)" .

p.435, italicised passage after para.2(3), line 1. Change "para.2(4)" to "para.3(3)(b)".

p.435, italicised passage after para.2(3), line 6. Change "para.2(5)" to "para.3(4)". SOCPA, Sch.8, para.3(4) then inserts a new sub-para.(3A):

"(3A) Where—
 (a) a designation applies this paragraph to any person ("the CSO"); and
 (b) by virtue of a designation under paragraph 1A the CSO has the power to impose a requirement under subparagraph (3) of that paragraph in relation to an offence under a relevant byelaw, the CSO shall also have any power a constable has under the relevant byelaw to remove a person from a place."

p.435, italicised passage after para.2(3). Sub-para.(3A) becomes sub-para.(3B).

p.435, n.17. Change "para.2(6)" to para.3(5)" and "or (3A)" to "or (3B)".

p.435, last italicised passage, in the line starting "(4A)" and in the penultimate line on the page. Change "(3A)" to "(3B)" .

p.436, sub-para.(5). Omit para.(a) (SOCPA Sch.8, para.3(6)).

p.436, n.18. Change "para.2(7)" to "para.3(6)" and "or (3A)" to "or (3B)".

p.436, sub-para.(6), the first italicised passage, line 2. Change "12(2)" to "13(2)".

p.436, in sub-para.(6), the first italicised passage, line 6. Change "2(8)" to "3(7)" and after para.(ac) insert new (ad):
"(ad) an offence under a relevant byelaw; or" (SOCPA, Sch.8, para.3(7)).

p.436, sub-para.(6), second italicised passage, line 1. Change "2(9)" to "3(8)". At the end of the italicised passage SOCPA, Sch.8, para.3(8) inserts new (6B)—(6F):

"(6B) In this paragraph "relevant byelaw" means a byelaw included in a list of byelaws which—

(a) have been made by a relevant body with authority to make byelaws for any place within the relevant police area; and

(b) the chief officer of the police force for the relevant police area and the relevant body have agreed to include in the list.

(6C) The list must be published by the chief officer in such a way as to bring it to the attention of members of the public in localities where the byelaws in the list apply.

(6D) A list of byelaws mentioned in sub-paragraph (6B) may be amended from time to time by agreement between the chief officer and the relevant body in question, by adding byelaws to it or removing byelaws from it, and the amended list shall also be published by the chief officer as mentioned in sub-paragraph (6C).

(6E) A relevant body for the purposes of sub-paragraph (6B) is—

(a) in England, a county council, a district council, a London borough council or a parish council; or in Wales, a county council, a county borough council or a community council;

(b) the Greater London Authority;

(c) Transport for London;

(d) a metropolitan county passenger transport authority established under section 28 of the Local Government Act 1985;

(e) any body specified in an order made by the Secretary of State.

(6F) An order under sub-paragraph (6E)(e) may provide, in relation to any body specified in the order, that the agreement mentioned in sub-paragraph (6B)(b) and (6D) is to be made between the chief officer and the Secretary of State (rather than between the chief officer and the relevant body)."

pp.436–437. Omit sub-para.(7) (SOCPA, Sch.8, para.3(9)).

p.437, after sub-para.(7). SOCPA, Sch.8, para.3(10) inserts new sub-para.(8):

"(8) The application of any provision of this paragraph by paragraph 3(2), 3A(2) or 7A(8) has no effect unless a designation under this paragraph has applied this paragraph to the CSO in question."

"Powers to search individuals and to seize and retain items: para.2A

p.437, line 3. Change "para.3" to "para.4"

p.437, italicised passage, line 4. Change "(3A)" to "(3B)"

p.437, para.3(2), line 3. Change "sub-paragraph (2)" to "paragraph 1A(3)" (SOCPA, Sch.8, para.5).

p.437, last full line. Change "para.4" to "para.6".

"Power to require name and address: road traffic offences: para.3A

p.438, italicised passage, new 3A(2), line 3. Change "sub-paragraph (2) of that paragraph" to "paragraph 1A(3)"

Power to use reasonable force to detain person: para.4

p.438 para.4(2)(b), after "relevant offences" insert "or relevant licensing offences" (SOCPA, Sch.9, para.3(a)); and in para.4(2)(3), after "making off" insert "and to keep him under control" (SOCPA, Sch.9, para.3(a)).

p.438, para.4(2)(b), after "paragraph" insert "1A or"; and in sub-para.(3) change "paragraph 2(2)" to "paragraph 1A(3)" (SOCPA, Sch.8, para.7).

p.438, n.21. Change "para.3" to "para.3(b)".

p.439, new para.4ZA, lines 2–3. Change "sub-paragraph (3A) of paragraph 2" to "paragraph 2(3B) or by virtue of paragraph 7A(8) or 7C(2)(a)".

p.439, new para.4ZA(b). Change "sub-paragraph (4) of paragraph 2" to "paragraph 2(4)".

Confiscation of tobacco etc.

p.440, after para.7. SOCPA, Sch.8, para.8 inserts new paras.7A, 7B and 7C:

"Search and seizure powers: alcohol and tobacco

  7A—(1) Where a designation applies this paragraph to any person ("the CSO"), the CSO shall have the powers set out below.

    (2) Where—

        (a) in exercise of the powers referred to in paragraph 5 or 6 the CSO has imposed, under section 12(2) of the Criminal Justice and Police Act 2001 or under section 1 of the Confiscation of Alcohol (Young Persons) Act 1997, a requirement on a person to surrender alcohol or a container for alcohol;

        (b) that person fails to comply with that requirement; and

        (c) the CSO reasonably believes that the person has alcohol or a container for alcohol in his possession,
        the CSO may search him for it.

(3) Where—

    (a) in exercise of the powers referred to in paragraph 7 the CSO has sought to seize something which by virtue of that paragraph he has a power to seize;

    (b) the person from whom he sought to seize it fails to surrender it; and

    (c) the CSO reasonably believes that the person has it in his possession,

    the CSO may search him for it.

(4) The power to search conferred by sub-paragraph (2) or (3)—

    (a) is to do so only to the extent that is reasonably required for the purpose of discovering whatever the CSO is searching for; and

    (b) does not authorise the CSO to require a person to remove any of his clothing in public other than an outer coat, jacket or gloves.

(5) A person who without reasonable excuse fails to consent to being searched is guilty of an offence and shall be liable, on summary conviction, to a fine not exceeding level 3 on the standard scale.

(6) A CSO who proposes to exercise the power to search a person under sub-paragraph (2) or (3) must inform him that failing without reasonable excuse to consent to being searched is an offence.

(7) If the person in question fails to consent to being searched, the CSO may require him to give the CSO his name and address.

(8) Sub-paragraph (3) of paragraph 2 applies in the case of a requirement imposed by virtue of sub-paragraph (7) as it applies in the case of a requirement under paragraph 1A(3); and sub-paragraphs (4) to (5) of paragraph 2 also apply accordingly.

(9) If on searching the person the CSO discovers what he is searching for, he may seize it and dispose of it.

Powers to seize and detain: controlled drugs

7B—(1) Where a designation applies this paragraph to any person ("the CSO"), the CSO shall, within the relevant police area, have the powers set out in sub-paragraphs (2) and (3).

(2) If the CSO—

    (a) finds a controlled drug in a person's possession (whether or not he finds it in the course of searching the person by virtue of a designation under any paragraph of this Schedule); and

    (b) reasonably believes that it is unlawful for the person to be in possession of it,

    the CSO may seize it and retain it.

(3) If the CSO—

    (a) finds a controlled drug in a person's possession (as mentioned in sub-paragraph (2)); or

    (b) reasonably believes that a person is in possession of a controlled drug, and reasonably believes that it is unlawful for the person to be in possession of it, the CSO may require him to give the CSO his name and address.

(4) If in exercise of the power conferred by sub-paragraph (2) the CSO seizes and retains a controlled drug, he must—

    (a) if the person from whom it was seized maintains that he was lawfully in possession of it, tell the person where inquiries about its recovery may be made; and

    (b) comply with a constable's instructions about what to do with it.

(5) A person who fails to comply with a requirement under subparagraph (3) is guilty of an offence and shall be liable, on summary conviction, to a fine not exceeding level 3 on the standard scale.

(6) In this paragraph, "controlled drug" has the same meaning as in the Misuse of Drugs Act 1971.

7C—(1) Sub-paragraph (2) applies where a designation applies this paragraph to any person ("the CSO").

(2) If the CSO imposes a requirement on a person under paragraph 7B(3)—

    (a) sub-paragraph (3) of paragraph 2 applies in the case of such a requirement as it applies in the case of a requirement under paragraph 1A(3); and

    (b) sub-paragraphs (4) to (5) of paragraph 2 also apply accordingly."

Confiscation of tobacco etc.: para.7

p.440, italicised passage, line 2. Change "para.12(3)" to "para.13(3)" and change "7A" to "7D".

Entry to save life or limb or prevent serious damage to property: para.8

p.441, italicised passage at the end of para.8, line 1. Change "para.5" to "para.9".

Power to stop bicycles

p.442, italicised passage after para.11A, line 1. Change "para.6" to "para.10".

Carrying out of road checks: para.13

p.443, italicised passage after para.13, line 1. Change "para.7" to "para.11".

Power to stop and search vehicles etc. in authorised areas: para.14

p.444, italicised passage after para.15, line 1. Change "para.8" to "para.12".

Power to modify paragraph 1(2)(a): para.15A

p.444, italicised passage after new para.15ZA, in the heading. Change "1(2)(a)" to "1(2A)" (SOCPA, s.122(3)(b)).

p.444, last italicised passage, line 1. Change "cl.113(3)(b)" to " s.122(3)(b)".

p.444, last italicised passage, after line 3 add at end. ", providing that the list contains only provisions mentioned in the first column of the Table in s.1(1) of the Criminal Justice and Police Act 2001".

PART 2

INVESTIGATING OFFICERS

Search warrants: para.16

p.445, n.25. Change "para.9(a)" to "para.13(a)".

p.445, n.26. Change "para.9(b)" to "para.13(b)".

p.446, italicised passage, line 1. Change "para.10" to "para.14".

Access to excluded and special procedure material: para.17

p.446, n.27. Change "para.11(a)" to "para.15(a)".

p.446, n.28. Change "para.11(b)" to "para.15(b)".

Power to transfer persons into custody of investigating officers: para.22

p.450, italicised passage, line 1. Change "para.5" to "para.6".

PART 3

DETENTION OFFICERS

Photographing persons in police detention: para.33

p.453, italicised passage, line 1. Change "Bill 2004–05" to "Act 2005" and change "para.12" to "para.16".

Taking of impressions of footwear: para.33A

p.454, line 8. Change "Bill 2004–05" to "Act 2005".

Powers in respect of detained persons: para.33B

p.454, after para.33C. The Drugs Act 2005, s.5(2) inserted a new para.33D:
   "33D. Where a designation applies this paragraph to any person, he is authorised to carry out the duty under—

   (a) section 55 of the Police and Criminal Evidence Act 1984 of informing
       a person who is to be subject to an intimate search under that section
       of the matters of which he is required to be informed in pursuance of
       subsection (3B) of that section;

   (b) section 55A of that Act of informing a person who is to be subject to
       x-ray or ultrasound (as the case may be) under that section of the mat-
       ters of which he is required to be informed in pursuance of subsection
       (3) of that section."

p.457, italicised passage, line 1. Change "cl.111(5)" to "s.120(5)".

PART 4A

STAFF CUSTODY OFFICERS

Powers in respect of detained persons: para.35B

p.458, after para.35B. The Drugs Act 2005, s.5 (2)(b) inserted a new paragraph
35C:
   "35C. Where a designation applies this paragraph to any person, he is authorised to carry out the duty under—

   (a) section 55 of the Police and Criminal Evidence Act 1984 of informing
       a person who is to be subject to an intimate search under that section
       of the matters of which he is required to be informed in pursuance of
       subsection (3B) of that section;

   (b) section 55A of that Act of informing a person who is to be subject to
       x-ray or ultrasound (as the case may be) under that section of the mat-
       ters of which he is required to be informed in pursuance of subsection
       (3) of that section."

p.458, n.39. Change "para.191" to "para.190".

p.458, n.40. Change "para 12(4)" to "para.13(4)" and change "section 139" to "section 162".

SCHEDULE 5

POWERS EXERCISABLE BY ACCREDITED PERSONS

p.459, n.41, 3 lines from the end. Change "cl.113(5)(a)" to s.122(5)(a)" and 2 lines from the end, change "cl.113(5)(b)" to "s.122(5)(b)". After "1967" insert: "s.1 of the Theft Act 1968, s.87 of the Environmental Protection Act 1990".

Power to require giving of name and address: para.2

p.460, first italicised passage, line 1. Change "Pt.1, para.14" to "Pt.2, para.18".

Power to require name and address of person acting in an anti-social manner: para.3

p.460, second italicised passage, line 1. Change "Pt.1, para.15" to "Pt.2, para.19".

Power to stop cycles: para.8A

p.462, italicised passage, line 1. Change "Pt.1, para.16" to "Pt.2, para.20".

Power to control traffic for purposes of escorting a load of exceptional dimensions: para.9

p.463, first italicised passage, line 1. Change "Pt.1, para.17" to "Pt.2, para.21".

Power to modify paragraph 1(2)(aa): para.9A

p.463, second italicised passage, the heading. Change "1(2)(aa)" to "1(2A)".

p.463, second italicised passage, line 1. Change "cl.113(6)" to "s.122(6)".

p.463, second italicised passage, line 3, add at end: ", providing that the list contains only provisions mentioned in the first column of the Table in section 1(1) of the Criminal Justice and Police Act 2001".

THE RIGHT TO SILENCE

CHAPTER 13

THE RIGHT TO SILENCE

THE CASE LAW ON THE RIGHT TO SILENCE AND THE RIGHT NOT TO INCRIMINATE ONESELF

Para.13–35, p.485, add new bullet point.
● *Previous convictions as a reason for silence.* Fear that giving evidence would result in his previous convictions becoming known to the jury does not give D protection against adverse inferences for failure to give evidence—*Becouarn* [2005] UKHL 55, [2005] 4 All E.R. 673 approving *Cowan* [1996] QB 373.

THE JUDGE'S DIRECTIONS TO THE JURY

Para.13–42, p.490, at the end. *Silence and legal advice.* For critical commentary on *Beckles* and on *Hoare and Pierce* see [2005] Crim.L.R. 562 and 568. See also B. Malik, *"Silence on legal advice: Clarity but not justice? R. v Beckles"*, [2005] 9 *International Journal of Evidence and Proof,* pp.211–16. For a case in which the conviction was quashed because of the trial judge's direction to the jury regarding silence and legal advice see *Bresa* [2005] EWCA Crim 1414.

POLICE AND CRIMINAL EVIDENCE ACT 1984

Unless otherwise indicated, the italicised passages showing the text of amendments to PACE in the Serious Organised Crime and Police Bill 2004–05 are confirmed and should be read as references to the Serious Organised Crime and Police Act 2005 (abbreviated "SOCPA"). The changes noted below mainly flow from a difference in the numbering between clauses of the Bill and sections of the Act.

PART I

POWERS TO STOP AND SEARCH

Power of constable to stop and search persons, vehicles etc.: s.1

p.527, n.2. Change "cl.106(2)" to "s.115(2)".

p.527, n.3. Change "cl.106(2)" to "s.115(3)".

p.527, n.4. Change "cl.106(3)" to "s.115(4)".

p.528, italicised passage, line 1. Change "cl.106(5)" to "s.115(5)".

Road checks: s.4

p.531, n.12. Change "para.8" to "para.43(2)"

PART II

POWERS OF ENTRY, SEARCH AND SEIZURE

Search warrants

Power of the justice of the peace to authorise entry and search of premises: s.8

p.534, italicised passage, line 1, line 1. Change "cl.104(4)" to "s.113(4)" and line 2, change "cl.105(2)" to "114(2)".

p.534, n.20. Change "para.8(3)" to "para.43(3)".

p.534, n.21. Change "cl.104(3)(a)" to "s.113(3)(a)".

p.534, n.22. Change "cl.104(3)(b)" to "s.113(3)(b)".

Search warrants—safeguards: s.15

p.538, s.15(2)(a). Move the word "and" from the end of sub-paragraph (1) to the end of sub-paragraph (ii) (SOCPA, s.114(4)(a), (b)).

p.538, first italicised passage, line 1. Change "cl.105(4)" to "s.114(4)".

p.538, n.28. Change "cl.104(6)" to "s.113(6)".

p.538, second italicised passage, line 1. Change "cl.104(7)" to "s.113(7)".
However, subs.(2A)(a) was replaced by: "(a) if the application relates to one or more sets of premises specified in the application, each set of premises which it is desired to enter and search;"[25]
In subs.(2A)(b) the words from the beginning to "Schedule 1 below", were replaced by: "if the application relates to any premises occupied or controlled by a person specified in the application—".[26]

p.539, n.29. Change "cl.105(5)" to "s.114(5)".

p.539, italicised passage after subs.(5), line 1. Change "cl.105(6)" to "s.114(6)".

p.539, italicised passage after subs.(6), line 1. Change "cl.104(8)" to "s.113(8)".

p.539, italicised passage after subs.(7), line 1. Change "cl.105(7)" to "s.114(7)".

Same para. The words "specific premises warrant (see section 8(1A)(a) above)" were replaced by "warrant"[27].

Execution of warrants: s.16

p.540, italicised passage, line 1. Change "cl.105(8)(a)" to "s.114(8)(a)".

p.540, italicised passage, line 2. change "Clause 104(9)(a)" to "s.113(9)(a)".

---

[25] The Serious Organised Crime and Police Act 2005 (Amendment) Order 2005, SI 2005/No.3496, para.7(2)(a).
[26] The Serious Organised Crime and Police Act 2005 (Amendment) Order 2005, SI 2005/No.3496, para.7(2)(b).
[27] The Serious Organised Crime and Police Act 2005 (Amendment) Order 2005, SI 2005/No.3496, para.7(3).

p.540, italicised passage, line 3. change "cl.105(8)(b)" to "s.114(8)(b)".

p.540, n.32. Change "cl.104(9)(b)" to "s.113(9)(b)". The words "specific premises" were removed by the Serious Organised Crime and Police Act 2005 (Amendment) Order 2005, SI 2005/No.3496, para.8.

p.541, italicised passage, line 1. Change "cl.105(8)" to "s.114(8)(c)".

p.541, s.16(12). SOCPA s.113(9)(c) deletes the word "the" before the word "premises".

Entry and search without search warrant

Entry for purpose of arrest etc.: s.17

p.541, n.36. Change "para.8(4)" to "para.43(4)".

p.542, para.(c)(iiia) of s.17 (1). SOCPA Sch.7, Pt.4, para.58(a) substitutes:

"(iiia) section 4 (driving etc. when under influence of drink or drugs) or 163 (failure to stop when required to do so by constable in uniform) of the Road Traffic Act 1988;

(iiib) section 27 of the Transport and Works Act 1992 (which relates to offences involving drink or drugs);"

p.542 after para.(ca) of s.17(1). SOCPA, Sch.7, Pt.4, para.58(b) inserts:

"(caa) of arresting a person for an offence to which section 61 of the Animal Health Act 1981 applies;".

Entry and search after arrest: s.18

p.543, n.46. Change "para.8(5)" to "para.43(5)".

p.548, italicised passage, line 1. Change "cl.101(1)" to "s.110(1)".

p.548, italicised passage, line 2. Change "Clause 101(5)" to "s.110(4)".

p.548, italicised passage, lines 2–3. Delete the sentence starting "Clause 101(4)"—this provision is not in the Act.

Fingerprinting of certain offenders: s.27

pp.550, the italicised passage after s.25(6). Change "cl.101(2)" to "s.110(2)".

Search upon arrest: s.32

p.555, italicised passage, line 1. Change "para.8(6)" to "para.43(6)".

PART IV

DETENTION

Detention—conditions and duration

Custody officers at police stations: s.36

p.558, line 1. Change "cl.112(2)" to "s.121(2)".

p.558, n.86. Change "cl.112(3)" to "s.121(3)".

p.558, n.89. Change "cl.112(4)" to "s.121(4)".

p.558, n.91. Change "cl.112(5)" to "s.121(5)".

p.559, line 3. Change "cl.112(6)" to "s.121(6)".

p.559–61, ss.37 to 37B. The provisions in these sections that refer to the DPP apply equally to the Director of Revenue and Customs Prosecutions. See the Commissioners for Revenue and Customs Act 2005, Sch.4, para.30.

Duties of custody officer before charge: s.37

p.560, s.37 after sub.(8). The Drugs Act 2005 inserts:
"(8A) Subsection (8B) applies if the offence for which the person is arrested is one in relation to which a sample could be taken under section 63B below and the custody officer—

(a) is required in pursuance of subsection (2) above to release the person arrested and decides to release him on bail, or

(b) decides in pursuance of subsection (7)(a) or (b) above to release the person without charge and on bail.

(8B) The detention of the person may be continued to enable a sample to be taken under section 63B, but this subsection does not permit a person to be detained for a period of more than 24 hours after the relevant time." (Drugs Act 2005, Sch.1, para.2)

Duties of custody officer after charge: s.38

p.563, s.38, subs.(1)(a)(iiia). The Drugs Act 2005 substitutes:
   "(iiia) in a case where a sample may be taken from the person under section 63B below, the custody officer has reasonable grounds for believing that the detention of the person is necessary to enable the sample to be taken from him;" (Drugs Act 2005, Sch.1, para.3(a))

p.564, s.38 (6A). In the definition of "minimum age" for "section 63B(3) below" substitute "section 63B(3)(b) below" (Drugs Act 2005, Sch.1, para.3(b)).

Responsibilities in relation to persons detained: s.39

p.565, n.21. Change "cl.112(7)" to "s.121(7)(a)".

p.565, italicised passage, line 1. Change "cl.112(7)(b)" to "s.121(7)(b)".

p.566, line 3. "officers" should read "officer".

Authorisation of continued detention: s.42

p.570, n.33. Change "para.8(7)" to "para.43(7)".

Warrants of further detention: s.43

p.572, n.37. Change "para.8(8)" to "para.43(8)".

PART V

QUESTIONING AND TREATMENT OF PERSONS BY POLICE

Intimate searches: s.55

p.584, s.55, after subs.(3). The Drugs Act 2005, s.3(2) inserted new subss.(3A) and (3B)[28]:

"(3A) A drug offence search shall not be carried out unless the appropriate consent has been given in writing.

(3B) Where it is proposed that a drug offence search be carried out, an appropriate officer shall inform the person who is to be subject to it—

    (a) of the giving of the authorisation for it; and
    (b) of the grounds for giving the authorisation."

p.585, s.55, after subs.(10). the Drugs Act 2005, s.3(3) inserted new subs.(10A)[29]:

"(10A) If the intimate search is a drug offence search, the custody record relating to that person shall also state—

    (a) the authorisation by virtue of which the search was carried out;
    (b) the grounds for giving the authorisation; and
    (c) the fact that the appropriate consent was given."

p.585, s.55(11). For "subsection (10)" the Drugs Act 2005 substitutes "subsections (10) and (10A)" (Drugs Act 2005, s.3(4)).

p.585, s.55, after subs.(13). the Drugs Act 2005, s 3(5) inserted new subs.(13A)[30]:

"(13A) Where the appropriate consent to a drug offence search of any person was refused without good cause, in any proceedings against that person for an offence—

---

[28] The equivalent provision in respect of Art.56 of the 1989 Northern Ireland PACE Order was made by the Drugs Act 2005, s.4 (2).
[29] The equivalent provision in respect of Art.56 of the 1989 Northern Ireland PACE Order was made by the Drugs Act 2005, s.4 (3).
[30] The equivalent provision in respect of Art.56 of the 1989 Northern Ireland PACE Order was made by the Drugs Act 2005, s.4 (5).

(a)   the court, in determining whether there is a case to answer;

(b)   a judge, in deciding whether to grant an application made by the accused under paragraph 2 of Schedule 3 to the Crime and Disorder Act 1998 (applications for dismissal); and

(c)   the court or jury, in determining whether that person is guilty of the offence charged,

may draw such inferences from the refusal as appear proper."

p.586, s.55(17). At the appropriate place the Drugs Act 2005, s.3(6) inserted:

"'appropriate officer' means—

(a)   a constable,

(b)   a person who is designated as a detention officer in pursuance of section 38 of the Police Reform Act 2002 if his designation applies paragraph 33D of Schedule 4 to that Act, or

(c)   a person designated as a staff officer in pursuance of section 38 of that Act if his designation applies paragraph 35C of Schedule 4 to that Act.

p.586, after s.55. the Drugs Act 2005, s.5 inserted a new s.55A:

"X-rays and ultrasound scans[31]:

55A—(1) If an officer of at least the rank of inspector has reasonable grounds for believing that a person who has been arrested for an offence and is in police detention—

(a)   may have swallowed a Class A drug, and

(b)   was in possession of it with the appropriate criminal intent before his arrest,

the officer may authorise that an x-ray is taken of the person or an ultrasound scan is carried out on the person (or both).

(2)   An x-ray must not be taken of a person and an ultrasound scan must not be carried out on him unless the appropriate consent has been given in writing.

(3)   If it is proposed that an x-ray is taken or an ultrasound scan is carried out, an appropriate officer must inform the person who is to be subject to it—

---

[31] The equivalent provision was inserted as Art. 56A of the 1989 Northern Ireland PACE Order by the Drugs Act 2005, s.6.

   (a) of the giving of the authorisation for it, and

   (b) of the grounds for giving the authorisation.

(4) An x-ray may be taken or an ultrasound scan carried out only by a suitably qualified person and only at—

   (a) a hospital,

   (b) a registered medical practitioner's surgery, or

   (c) some other place used for medical purposes.

(5) The custody record of the person must also state—

   (a) the authorisation by virtue of which the x-ray was taken or the ultrasound scan was carried out,

   (b) the grounds for giving the authorisation, and

   (c) the fact that the appropriate consent was given.

(6) The information required to be recorded by subsection (5) must be recorded as soon as practicable after the x-ray has been taken or ultrasound scan carried out (as the case may be).

(7) Every annual report—

   (a) under section 22 of the Police Act 1996, or

   (b) made by the Commissioner of Police of the Metropolis,

must contain information about x-rays which have been taken and ultrasound scans which have been carried out under this section in the area to which the report relates during the period to which it relates.

(8) The information about such x-rays and ultrasound scans must be presented separately and must include—

   (a) the total number of x-rays;

   (b) the total number of ultrasound scans;

   (c) the results of the x-rays;

   (d) the results of the ultrasound scans.

(9) If the appropriate consent to an x-ray or ultrasound scan of any person is refused without good cause, in any proceedings against that person for an offence—

   (a) the court, in determining whether there is a case to answer,

   (b) a judge, in deciding whether to grant an application made by the accused under paragraph 2 of Schedule 3 to the Crime and Disorder Act 1998 (applications for dismissal), and

   (c) the court or jury, in determining whether that person is guilty of the offence charged,

may draw such inferences from the refusal as appear proper.

(10) In this section "the appropriate criminal intent", "appropriate officer", "Class A drug" and "suitably qualified person" have the same meanings as in section 55 above."

Right to have someone informed when arrested: s.56

p.586, nn.81 and 84. Change "para.8(9)(a)" to "para.43(9)(a)".

p.587, n.85, line 4. Change "Sch.8(9)(b)" to "Sch.7, para.43(9)(b)".

Access to legal advice: s.58

pp.588–89, nn.89 and 91. Change "para.8(10)(a)" to "para.43(10(a)".`

p.589, n.92, line 4. Change "para.8(10)(b)" to "para.43(10(b)".

Fingerprinting: s.61

p.591, italicised passage, line 1. Change "cl.108(2)" to "s.117(2)".

p.592, n.10. Change "cl.108(3)" to "s.117(3)".

p.592, notes 11 and 12. Change "cl.108(4)" to "s.117(4)" .

p.593, italicised passage, line 1. Change "cl.109(2)" to "s.118(2)".

Fingerprints and samples—supplementary provisions: s.63A

p.598, n.58. Change "cl.109(3)" to "s.118(3)".

p.599, italicised passage, line 1. Change "cl.108(5)" to "s.117(5)(a)".

p.599, n.60. Change "cl.108(5)(b)" to "s.117(5)(b)".

p.600, s.63A(1C). In para.(a), after "fingerprints" insert ", impressions of footwear"; (ii) in para.(b), after "fingerprints" insert ", of the impressions of footwear"; (iii) after the third "fingerprints" insert "or impressions of footwear"; (iv) after the fourth "fingerprints" insert ", impressions of footwear". (SOCPA, s.118(3)(b).)

Testing for the presence of Class A drugs: s.63B

p.601, s.63B. The Drugs Act 2005 amends s.63B in accordance with subs.(2) to (12):

- In sub.(1) for "the following conditions are met" substitute "—

  (a) either the arrest condition or the charge condition is met;

  (b) both the age condition and the request condition are met; and

  (c) the notification condition is met in relation to the arrest condition, the charge condition or the age condition (as the case may be)." (Drugs Act 2005, s.7(2))

- After subs.(1) insert (1A):

  "(1A) The arrest condition is that the person concerned has been arrested for an offence but has not been charged with that offence and either—
    (a) the offence is a trigger offence; or
    (b) a police officer of at least the rank of inspector has reasonable grounds for suspecting that the misuse by that person of a specified Class A drug caused or contributed to the offence and has authorised the sample to be taken". (Drugs Act 2005, s.7(3).)

- In subs.(2), for "The first condition is" substitute "The charge condition is either" (Drugs Act 2005, s.7(4)).
- For subs.(3) substitute:

  "(3) The age condition is—
    (a) if the arrest condition is met, that the person concerned has attained the age of 18;
    (b) if the charge condition is met, that he has attained the age of 14." (Drugs Act 2005, s.7 (5).)

- In subs.(4), for "third" substitute "request" (Drugs Act 2005, s.7(6)).
- After subs.(4) insert subss.(4A) and (4B):

"(4A) The notification condition is that—

- (a) the relevant chief officer has been notified by the Secretary of State that appropriate arrangements have been made for the police area as a whole, or for the particular police station, in which the person is in police detention, and
- (b) the notice has not been withdrawn.

(4B) For the purposes of subsection (4A) above, appropriate arrangements are arrangements for the taking of samples under this section from whichever of the following is specified in the notification—

- (a) persons in respect of whom the arrest condition is met;
- (b) persons in respect of whom the charge condition is met;
- (c) persons who have not attained the age of 18." (Drugs Act 2005, s.7(7).)

- In subs.(5)(b) after "subsection" insert "(1A)(b) or" (Drugs Act 2005, s.7(8)).
- After subs.(5A) insert subss.(5B), (5C) and (5D):

"(5B) If a sample is taken under this section from a person in respect of whom the arrest condition is met no other sample may be taken from him under this section during the same continuous period of detention but—

- (a) if the charge condition is also met in respect of him at any time during that period, the sample must be treated as a sample taken by virtue of the fact that the charge condition is met;
- (b) the fact that the sample is to be so treated must be recorded in the person's custody record.

(5C) Despite subsection (1)(a) above, a sample may be taken from a person under this section if—

- (a) he was arrested for an offence (the first offence),
- (b) the arrest condition is met but the charge condition is not met,
- (c) before a sample is taken by virtue of subsection (1) above he would (but for his arrest as mentioned in paragraph (d) below) be required to be released from police detention,
- (d) he continues to be in police detention by virtue of his having been arrested for an offence not falling within subsection (1A) above, and
- (e) the sample is taken before the end of the period of 24 hours starting with the time when his detention by virtue of his arrest for the first offence began.

(5D) A sample must not be taken from a person under this section if he is detained in a police station unless he has been brought before the custody officer." (Drugs Act 2005, s.7(9).)

- For subs.(6A) substitute:

> "(6A) The Secretary of State may by order made by statutory instrument amend—
>> (a) paragraph (a) of subsection (3) above, by substituting for the age for the time being specified a different age specified in the order, or different ages so specified for different police areas so specified;
>> (b) paragraph (b) of that subsection, by substituting for the age for the time being specified a different age specified in the order." (Drugs Act 2005, s.7(10).)

- In subs.(7), after para.(a) insert (aa):

> "(aa) for the purpose of informing any decision about the giving of a conditional caution under Part 3 of the Criminal Justice Act 2003 to the person concerned;" (Drugs Act 2005, s.7(11)).

- Subs.(9) is omitted (Drugs Act 2005, s.7(12).
- Subs.(13) provides that on the day s.7 comes into force [January 1, 2006] the "notification condition" must be treated as being met—

> "(a) for the purposes of the charge condition in relation to a police area, if subsection (2) of section 63B of PACE is in force immediately before that day in relation to the police area;
>
> (b) for the purposes of the age condition in relation to a police area or police station, if before that day notification was given under subsection (9) of that section in relation to the police area or police station and was not withdrawn,

> and "age condition", "charge condition" and "notification condition" have the same meaning as in section 63B of PACE (as amended by this section)."
- Subs.(14) provides that subsection (13) does not prevent the Secretary of State withdrawing a notification which is treated as made by virtue of that subsection.

p.602, s.63B(7). After paragraph (c) insert (ca) and (cb):
"(ca) for the purpose of an assessment which the person concerned is required to attend by virtue of section 9(2) or 10(2) of the Drugs Act 2005;
(cb) for the purpose of proceedings against the person concerned for an offence under section 12(3) or 14(3) of that Act;" (Drugs Act 2005, Sch.1, para.4).

p.602, s.63B(9). Repealed. (Drugs Act 2005, Sch.2).

Testing for presence of Class A drugs—supplementary: s.63C

p.603 after s.63C. Part 3 of the Drugs Act 2005 establishes a new system for 'Initial assessment' and 'Follow up assessment" of misuse of drugs. This new system is a development from the provisions of ss.63B and 63C of PACE. For that reason the whole of Part 3 is included here (italicised):

"PART 3

ASSESSMENT OF MISUSE OF DRUGS

9. Initial assessment following testing for presence of Class A drugs

(1) This section applies if—
   (a) a sample is taken under section 63B of PACE (testing for presence of Class A drug) from a person detained at a police station,
   (b) an analysis of the sample reveals that a specified Class A drug may be present in the person's body,
   (c) the age condition is met, and
   (d) the notification condition is met.

(2) A police officer may, at any time before the person is released from detention at the police station, require him to attend an initial assessment and remain for its duration.

(3) An initial assessment is an appointment with a suitably qualified person (an "initial assessor")—
   (a) for the purpose of establishing whether the person is dependent upon or has a propensity to misuse any specified Class A drug,
   (b) if the initial assessor thinks that he has such a dependency or propensity, for the purpose of establishing whether he might benefit from further assessment, or from assistance or treatment (or both), in connection with the dependency or propensity, and
   (c) if the initial assessor thinks that he might benefit from such assistance or treatment (or both), for the purpose of providing him with advice, including an explanation of the types of assistance or treatment (or both) which are available.

(4) The age condition is met if the person has attained the age of 18 or such different age as the Secretary of State may by order made by statutory instrument specify for the purposes of this section.

(5) In relation to a person ("A") who has attained the age of 18, the notification condition is met if—
   (a) the relevant chief officer has been notified by the Secretary of State that arrangements for conducting initial assessments for persons who have attained the age of 18 have been made for persons from whom samples have been taken (under section 63B of PACE) at the police station in which A is detained, and
   (b) the notice has not been withdrawn.

(6) In relation to a person ("C") who is of an age which is less than 18, the notification condition is met if—

    (a) the relevant chief officer has been notified by the Secretary of State that arrangements for conducting initial assessments for persons of that age have been made for persons from whom samples have been taken (under section 63B of PACE) at the police station in which C is detained, and

    (b) the notice has not been withdrawn.

(7) In subsections (5) and (6), "relevant chief officer" means the chief officer of police of the police force for the police area in which the police station is situated.

10. Follow-up assessment

(1) This section applies if—

    (a) a police officer requires a person to attend an initial assessment and remain for its duration under section 9(2),

    (b) the age condition is met, and

    (c) the notification condition is met.

(2) The police officer must, at the same time as he imposes the requirement under section 9(2)—

    (a) require the person to attend a follow-up assessment and remain for its duration, and

    (b) inform him that the requirement ceases to have effect if he is informed at the initial assessment that he is no longer required to attend the follow-up assessment.

(3) A follow-up assessment is an appointment with a suitably qualified person (a "follow-up assessor")—

    (a) for any of the purposes of the initial assessment which were not fulfilled at the initial assessment, and

    (b) if the follow-up assessor thinks it appropriate, for the purpose of drawing up a care plan.

(4) A care plan is a plan which sets out the nature of the assistance or treatment (or both) which may be most appropriate for the person in connection with any dependency upon, or any propensity to misuse, a specified Class A drug which the follow-up assessor thinks that he has.

(5) The age condition is met if the person has attained the age of 18 or such different age as the Secretary of State may by order made by statutory instrument specify for the purposes of this section.

(6) In relation to a person ("A") who has attained the age of 18, the notification condition is met if—

    (a) the relevant chief officer has been notified by the Secretary of State that arrangements for conducting follow-up assessments for persons who have attained the age of 18 have been made for persons from whom samples have been taken (under section 63B of PACE) at the police station in which A is detained, and

    (b) the notice has not been withdrawn.

(7) In relation to a person ("C") who is of an age which is less than 18, the notification condition is met if—

(a)   the relevant chief officer has been notified by the Secretary of State that arrangements for conducting follow-up assessments for persons of that age have been made for persons from whom samples have been taken (under section 63B of PACE) at the police station in which C is detained, and

(b)   the notice has not been withdrawn.

(8) In subsections (6) and (7), "relevant chief officer" means the chief officer of police of the police force for the police area in which the police station is situated.

11. Requirements under sections 9 and 10: supplemental

(1) This section applies if a person is required to attend an initial assessment and remain for its duration by virtue of section 9(2).

(2) A police officer must—

(a)   inform the person of the time when, and the place at which, the initial assessment is to take place, and

(b)   explain that this information will be confirmed in writing.

(3) A police officer must warn the person that he may be liable to prosecution if he fails without good cause to attend the initial assessment and remain for its duration.

(4) If the person is also required to attend a follow-up assessment and remain for its duration by virtue of section 10(2), a police officer must also warn the person that he may be liable to prosecution if he fails without good cause to attend the follow-up assessment and remain for its duration.

(5) A police officer must give the person notice in writing which—

(a)   confirms that he is required to attend and remain for the duration of an initial assessment or both an initial assessment and a follow-up assessment (as the case may be),

(b)   confirms the information given in pursuance of subsection (2), and

(c)   repeats the warning given in pursuance of subsection (3) and any warning given in pursuance of subsection (4).

(6) The duties imposed by subsections (2) to (5) must be discharged before the person is released from detention at the police station.

(7) A record must be made, as part of the person's custody record, of—

(a)   the requirement imposed on him by virtue of section 9(2),

(b)   any requirement imposed on him by virtue of section 10(2),

(c)   the information and explanation given to him in pursuance of subsection (2) above,

(d)   the warning given to him in pursuance of subsection (3) above and any warning given to him in pursuance of subsection (4) above, and

(e)   the notice given to him in pursuance of subsection (5) above.

(8) If a person is given a notice in pursuance of subsection (5), a police officer or a suitably qualified person may give the person a further notice in writing which—

(a)   informs the person of any change to the time when, or to the place at which, the initial assessment is to take place, and

(b)   repeats the warning given in pursuance of subsection (3) and any warning given in pursuance of subsection (4).

12. Attendance at initial assessment

(1) This section applies if a person is required to attend an initial assessment and remain for its duration by virtue of section 9(2).

(2) The initial assessor must inform a police officer or a police support officer if the person—

    (a) *fails to attend the initial assessment at the specified time and place, or*

    (b) *attends the assessment at the specified time and place but fails to remain for its duration.*

(3) A person is guilty of an offence if without good cause—

    (a) *he fails to attend an initial assessment at the specified time and place, or*

    (b) *he attends the assessment at the specified time and place but fails to remain for its duration.*

(4) A person who is guilty of an offence under subsection (3) is liable on summary conviction to imprisonment for a term not exceeding 51 weeks, or to a fine not exceeding level 4 on the standard scale, or to both.

(5) If a person fails to attend an initial assessment at the specified time and place, any requirement imposed on him by virtue of section 10(2) ceases to have effect.

(6) In this section—

    (a) *the specified time, in relation to the person concerned, is the time specified in the notice given to him in pursuance of subsection (5) of section 11 or, if a further notice specifying a different time has been given to him in pursuance of subsection (8) of that section, the time specified in that notice, and*

    (b) *the specified place, in relation to the person concerned, is the place specified in the notice given to him in pursuance of subsection (5) of section 11 or, if a further notice specifying a different place has been given to him in pursuance of subsection (8) of that section, the place specified in that notice.*

(7) In relation to an offence committed before the commencement of section 281(5) of the Criminal Justice Act 2003 (c. 44) (alteration of penalties for summary offences), the reference in subsection (4) to 51 weeks is to be read as a reference to 3 months.

13. Arrangements for follow-up assessment

(1) This section applies if—

    (a) *a person attends an initial assessment in pursuance of section 9(2), and*

    (b) *he is required to attend a follow-up assessment and remain for its duration by virtue of section 10(2).*

(2) If the initial assessor thinks that a follow-up assessment is not appropriate, he must inform the person concerned that he is no longer required to attend the follow-up assessment.

(3) The requirement imposed by virtue of section 10(2) ceases to have effect if the person is informed as mentioned in subsection (2).

(4) If the initial assessor thinks that a follow-up assessment is appropriate, the assessor must—

(a) inform the person of the time when, and the place at which, the follow-up assessment is to take place, and

(b) explain that this information will be confirmed in writing.

(5) The assessor must also warn the person that, if he fails without good cause to attend the follow-up assessment and remain for its duration, he may be liable to prosecution.

(6) The initial assessor must also give the person notice in writing which—

(a) confirms that he is required to attend and remain for the duration of the follow-up assessment,

(b) confirms the information given in pursuance of subsection (4), and

(c) repeats the warning given in pursuance of subsection (5).

(7) The duties mentioned in subsections (2) and (4) to (6) must be discharged before the conclusion of the initial assessment.

(8) If a person is given a notice in pursuance of subsection (6), the initial assessor or another suitably qualified person may give the person a further notice in writing which—

(a) informs the person of any change to the time when, or to the place at which, the follow-up assessment is to take place, and

(b) repeats the warning mentioned in subsection (5).

14. Attendance at follow-up assessment

(1) This section applies if a person is required to attend a follow-up assessment and remain for its duration by virtue of section 10(2).

(2) The follow-up assessor must inform a police officer or a police support officer if the person—

(a) fails to attend the follow-up assessment at the specified time and place, or

(b) attends the assessment at the specified time and place but fails to remain for its duration.

(3) A person is guilty of an offence if without good cause—

(a) he fails to attend a follow-up assessment at the specified time and place, or

(b) he attends the assessment at the specified time and place but fails to remain for its duration.

(4) A person who is guilty of an offence under subsection (3) is liable on summary conviction to imprisonment for a term not exceeding 51 weeks, or to a fine not exceeding level 4 on the standard scale, or to both.

(5) In this section—

(a) the specified time, in relation to the person concerned, is the time specified in the notice given to him in pursuance of subsection (6) of section 13 or, if a further notice specifying a different time has been given to him in pursuance of subsection (8) of that section, the time specified in that notice, and

(b) the specified place, in relation to the person concerned, is the place specified in the notice given to him in pursuance of subsection (6) of section 13 or, if a further notice specifying a different place has been given to him in pursuance of subsection (8) of that section, the place specified in that notice.

(6) In relation to an offence committed before the commencement of section 281(5) of the Criminal Justice Act 2003 (c. 44) (alteration of penalties for summary offences), the reference in subsection (4) to 51 weeks is to be read as a reference to 3 months.

15. Disclosure of information about assessments

(1) An initial assessor may disclose information obtained as a result of an initial assessment to any of the following—
- (a) a person who is involved in the conduct of the assessment;
- (b) a person who is or may be involved in the conduct of any follow-up assessment.

(2) A follow-up assessor may disclose information obtained as a result of a follow-up assessment to a person who is involved in the conduct of the assessment.

(3) Subject to subsections (1) and (2), information obtained as a result of an initial or a follow-up assessment may not be disclosed by any person without the written consent of the person to whom the assessment relates.

(4) Nothing in this section affects the operation of section 17(4).

16. Samples submitted for further analysis

(1) A requirement imposed on a person by virtue of section 9(2) or 10(2) ceases to have effect if at any time before he has fully complied with the requirement—
- (a) a police officer makes arrangements for a further analysis of the sample taken from him as mentioned in section 9(1)(a), and
- (b) the analysis does not reveal that a specified Class A drug was present in the person's body.

(2) If a requirement ceases to have effect by virtue of subsection (1), a police officer must so inform the person concerned.

(3) Nothing in subsection (1) affects the validity of anything done in connection with the requirement before it ceases to have effect.

(4) If a person fails to attend an assessment which he is required to attend by virtue of section 9(2) or fails to remain for the duration of such an assessment but, at any time after his failure, the requirement ceases to have effect by virtue of subsection (1) above—
- (a) no proceedings for an offence under section 12(3) may be brought against him, and
- (b) if any such proceedings were commenced before the requirement ceased to have effect, those proceedings must be discontinued.

(5) If a person fails to attend an assessment which he is required to attend by virtue of section 10(2) or fails to remain for the duration of such an assessment but, at any time after his failure, the requirement ceases to have effect by virtue of subsection (1) above—
- (a) no proceedings for an offence under section 14(3) may be brought against him, and
- (c) if any such proceedings were commenced before the requirement ceased to have effect, those proceedings must be discontinued.

17. Relationship with Bail Act 1976 etc.

(1) A requirement imposed on a person by virtue of section 9(2) or 10(2) ceases to have effect if at any time before he has fully complied with the requirement—
   (a)   he is charged with the related offence, and
   (b)   a court imposes on him a condition of bail under section 3(6D) of the Bail Act 1976 (c. 63) (duty to impose condition to undergo relevant assessment etc.).

(2) For the purposes of section 3(6D) of the 1976 Act, a relevant assessment (within the meaning of that Act) is to be treated as having been carried out if—
   (a)   a person attends an initial assessment and remains for its duration, and
   (b)   the initial assessor is satisfied that the initial assessment fulfilled the purposes of a relevant assessment.

(3) For the purposes of paragraph 6B(2)(b) of Schedule 1 to the 1976 Act (exceptions to right to bail for drug users in certain areas), a person is to be treated as having undergone a relevant assessment (within the meaning of that Act) if—
   (a)   the person attends an initial assessment and remains for its duration, and
   (b)   the initial assessor is satisfied that the initial assessment fulfilled the purposes of a relevant assessment.

(4) An initial assessor may disclose information relating to an initial assessment for the purpose of enabling a court considering an application for bail by the person concerned to determine whether subsection (2) or (3) applies.

(5) Nothing in subsection (1) affects—
   (a)   the validity of anything done in connection with the requirement before it ceases to have effect, or
   (b)   any liability which the person may have for an offence under section 12(3) or 14(3) committed before the requirement ceases to have effect.

(6) In subsection (1), "the related offence" is the offence in respect of which the condition specified in subsection (1A) or (2) of section 63B of PACE is satisfied in relation to the taking of the sample mentioned in section 9(1)(a) of this Act.

18. Orders under this Part and guidance

(1) A statutory instrument containing an order under section 9(4) or 10(5) must not be made unless a draft of the instrument has been laid before, and approved by a resolution of, each House of Parliament.

(2) Any such order may—

   (a)   make different provision for different police areas;

   (b)   make such provision as the Secretary of State considers appropriate in connection with requiring persons who have not attained the age of 18 to attend and remain for the duration of an initial assessment or a follow-up assessment (as the case may be), including provision amending this Part.

(3) In exercising any functions conferred by this Part, a police officer and a suitably qualified person must have regard to any guidance issued by the Secretary of State for the purposes of this Part.

19. Interpretation

(1) This section applies for the purposes of this Part.

(2) "Class A drug" and "misuse" have the same meanings as in the Misuse of Drugs Act 1971 (c. 38).

(3) "Specified", in relation to a Class A drug, has the same meaning as in Part 3 of the Criminal Justice and Court Services Act 2000 (c. 43).

(4) "Initial assessment" and "initial assessor" must be construed in accordance with section 9(3).

(5) "Follow-up assessment" and "follow-up assessor" must be construed in accordance with section 10(3).

(6) "Suitably qualified person" means a person who has such qualifications or experience as are from time to time specified by the Secretary of State for the purposes of this Part.

(7) "Police support officer" means a person who is employed by a police authority under section 15(1) of the Police Act 1996 (c. 16) and who is under the direction and control of the chief officer of police of the police force maintained by that authority.

(8) "PACE" means the Police and Criminal Evidence Act 1984 (c. 60)."

Destruction of fingerprints and samples: s.64

p.604, s.64(1A). Change "or the conduct of a prosecution" to ", the conduct of a prosecution or the identification of a deceased person or of the person from whom a body part came". (SOCPA, s.117(7)).

p.604, italicised passage, line 1. Change "cl.108(7)" to "s.117(8)".

p.604, n.72. Change "cl.109(4)" to "s.118(4)".

p.605, n.75. Change "cl.108(8)" to "s.117(9)"

p.605, n.76. Change "cl.108(9)(a)" to "s.117(10)(a)".

p.605, n.77. Change "cl.108(9)(b)" to "s.117(10)(b)".

Photographing of suspects etc.: s.64A

p.606, italicised passage, line 1. Change "cl.107(2)" to "s.116(2)".

p.606, subs.(1B)(c), line 2. Change "(3A)" to "(3B)"

p.607, s.64A(4)(a), line 3, after "prosecution". Insert "or to the enforcement of a sentence" (SOCPA, s.116(3)).

p.607, s.64A(5) after para.(b). Insert "; and (c) 'sentence' includes any order made by a court in England and Wales when dealing with an offender in respect of his offence." (SOCPA, s.116(4)).

p.607, 3 lines from bottom of page. Change "cl.107(3)" to "s.116(5)".

Fingerprints and samples—supplementary: s.65

p.608, italicised passage, line 1. Change "cl.110(2)" to "s.119(2)".

p.609, italicised passage, line 1. Change "cl.110(2)" to "s.119(3)".

PART VI

CODES OF PRACTICE—GENERAL

Codes of Practice: s.66

p.610, s.66, (i). Move "or" to end of (ii) (SOCPA, s.110(3)(a)).

p.610, s.66(1)(a) italicised passage, line 1. Change "cl.101(3)" to "s.110(3)".

PART XI

MISCELLANEOUS AND SUPPLEMENTARY

Application of Act to Customs and Excise: s.114

p.625, s.114(4). Repealed by the Commissioners for Revenue and Customs Act 2005, Sch.4, para.31. (For the equivalent repeal of Art.85(3) of the 1989 Northern Ireland PACE Order see Sch.4, para.40 of the same Act.)

Power to apply Act to officers of the Secretary of State: s.114A

p.626, n.70. Change "para.8(11)" to "para.43(11)".

Meaning of "serious arrestable offence": s.116

p.626, s.116, italicised passage, line 1. Change "para.8(12)" to "para.43(12)".

General interpretation: s.118

p.627, n.76. Change "para.2(2)" to "para.24(2)".

SCHEDULES

Schedule 1

SPECIAL PROCEDURE

Making of orders by circuit [judge]: para.1

p.631, n.2. Change "para.8(13)" to "para.43(13)".

p.631, n.2a. Change "cl.104(11)" to "s.113(11)".

p.631, para.3(b), line 1. Change "the premises" to "such premises" (SOCPA, s.113(12)).

Issue of warrants by a judge: para.12

p.633, n.6. Change "cl.104(13)(a)" to "s.113(13)(a)".

p.633, n.7. Change "cl.104(13)(b)" to "s.113(13)(b)".

p.633, italicised passage, line 1. Change "cl.104(14)" to "s.113(14)".

p.633, n.8. Change "cl.104(15)" to "s.113(15)".

Costs: para.17

p.634, n.9. Change "cl.105(9)" to "s.114(9)".

Schedule 1A

p.634, n.10. Change "para.2(3)" to "para.24(3)".

Schedule 2

PRESERVED POWERS OF ARREST

p.638. SOCPA, Sch.7, Pt.1, para.24(4) removed the entries relating to: the Military Lands Act 1892; the Protection of Animals Act 1911; the Public Order Act 1936; the Street Offences Act 1959; the Criminal Law Act 1977; and the Animal Health Act 1981.

Schedule 5

SERIOUS ARRESTABLE OFFENCES

p.639, italicised passage. Change "para.8(14)" to "para.43(14)".

Schedule 6

CONSEQUENTIAL AMENDMENTS

PART I

ENGLAND AND WALES

Criminal Law Act 1967 (c.58)

p.644, the italicised passage, line 1. Change "Sch.16, Pt.2" to "Sch.17, Pt.2".

CODES OF PRACTICE

CODE A

CODE OF PRACTICE FOR THE EXERCISE BY: POLICE OFFICERS OF STATUTORY POWERS OF STOP AND SEARCH AND POLICE OFFICERS AND POLICE STAFF OF REQUIREMENTS TO RECORD PUBLIC ENCOUNTERS

Commencement—transitional arrangements

p.662. Delete paragraph and replace with:
"This code applies to any search by a police officer and the requirement to record public encounters taking place after midnight on December 31, 2005."

2 Explanation of powers to stop and search

A 2.1(d). Change reference from Code B "2.3a" to "2.4"

Searches requiring reasonable grounds for suspicion

A 2.2. Add at end: "A person's religion cannot be considered as reasonable grounds for suspicion and should never be considered as a reason to stop or stop and search an individual."

A 1. At the end add: "[See Note 21]"

Recording requirements

A 4.3(iii). "[See Note 17]" should read "[See Note 16]"

A 4.4. After "4.3(x)" add "or 4.10A"

A 4.7, at end. Change to ". . .a record must still be made in accordance with the procedure outlined in Paragraph 4.12".

A 4.10. Add:
"4.10A When an officer makes a record of the stop electronically and is unable to produce a copy of the form at the time, the officer must explain how the person can obtain a full copy of the record of the stop or search and give the person a receipt which contains:

- a unique reference number and guidance on how to obtain a full copy of the stop or search;

- the name of the officer who carried out the stop or search (unless *paragraph 4.4* applies); and

- the power used to stop and search them. [See *Note 21*]"

Recording of encounters not governed by statutory powers

A 4.11. Delete existing para.4.11 and replace with "Not used"

A 4.14. Change 4.14 to:
"A separate record need not be completed when:

- stopping a person in a vehicle when an HORT/1 form, a Vehicle Defect Rectification Scheme Notice, or a Fixed Penalty Notice is issued. It also does not apply when a specimen of breath is required under Section 6 of the Road Traffic Act 1988.

- stopping a person when a Penalty Notice is issued for an offence."

A 4.17(iii). "[See Note 18]" should read "[See Note 17]".

A 4.17(iv). "[See Note 19]" should read "[See Note 18]".

A 4.18. "[See Note 19]" should read "[See Note 18]".

A 4.19. Delete ". . .a person requests it, regardless of whether the officer considers that. . .". Delete "If the form was requested when the officer does not believe the criteria were met, this should be recorded on the form." and replace with "If the criteria are not met but the person requests a record, the officer should provide a copy of the form but record on it that the encounter did not meet the criteria. The officer can refuse to issue the form if he or she reasonably believes that the purpose of the request is deliberately aimed at frustrating or delaying legitimate police activity. [See Note 20]"

Notes for guidance

Recording

A GN 20. Add new Guidance Notes 20 and 21:
"*20 Where an officer engages in conversation which is not pertinent to the actions or whereabouts of the individual (e.g. does not relate to why the person is there, what they are doing or where they have been or are going) then issuing a form would not meet the criteria set out in paragraph 4.12. Situations designed to impede police activity may arise, for example, in public order situations where individuals engage in dialogue with the officer but the officer does not initiate or engage in contact about the person's individual circumstances.*

21 In situations where it is not practicable to provide a written record of the stop or stop and search at that time, the officer should consider providing the person with details of the station to which the person may attend for a record. This may take the form of a simple business card, adding the date of the stop or stop and search."

ANNEX A

SUMMARY OF MAIN STOP AND SEARCH POWERS

Add under title but before table "This table relates to stop and search powers only. Individual statutes below may contain other police powers of entry, search and seizure."

p.678, item 6, Object of search column. After "not exceeding 3 inches, prohibited possession of a category 4 (display grade) firework, any person under 18", add "in possession of an adult firework in a public place)".

p.681 after Annex B. Insert new Annex C.

"ANNEX C

SUMMARY OF POWERS OF COMMUNITY SUPPORT OFFICERS TO
SEARCH AND SEIZE

The following is a summary of the search and seizure powers that may be exercised by a community support officer (CSO) who has been designated with the relevant powers in accordance with Part 4 of the Police Reform Act 2002.

When exercising any of these powers, a CSO must have regard to any relevant provisions of this Code, including section 3 governing the conduct of searches and the steps to be taken prior to a search.

Power to stop and search not requiring consent

Designation	Power conferred	Object of search	Extent of search	Where Exercisable
Police Reform Act 2002, Sched.4, para.15	(a) Terrorism Act 2000, s.44(1)(a) and (d) and 45(2);	Items intended to be used in connection with terrorism.	(a) Vehicles or anything carried in or on the vehicle and anything carried by driver or passenger.	Anywhere within area of locality authorised and in the company and under the supervision of a constable.
	(b) Terrorism Act 2000, s.44 (2)(b) and 45(2).		(b) Anything carried by a pedestrian.	

1. Powers to search requiring the consent of the person and seizure

A CSO may detain a person using reasonable force where necessary as set out in Part 1 of Schedule 4 to the Police Reform Act 2002. If the person has been lawfully detained, the CSO may search the person provided that person gives consent to such a search in relation to the following:

Designation	Power conferred	Object of search	Extent of search	Where Exercisable
Police Reform Act 2002, Sched.4, para.7A	(a) Criminal Justice and Police Act 2001, s.12(2)	(a) Alcohol or a container for alcohol	(a) Persons	(a) Designated public place
	(b) Confiscation of Alcohol (Young Persons) Act 1997, s.1	(b) Alcohol	(b) Persons under 18 years old	(b) Public place
	(c) Children and Young Persons Act 1933, s.7(3)	(c) Tobacco or cigarette papers	(c) Persons under 16 years old found smoking	(c) Public place

2. Powers to search not requiring the consent of the person and seizure

A CSO may detain a person using reasonable force where necessary as set out in Part 1 of Schedule 4 to the Police Reform Act 2002. If the person has been lawfully detained, the CSO may search the person without the need for that person's consent in relation to the following:

Designation	Power conferred	Object of search	Extent of search	Where Exercisable
Police Reform Act 2002, Sch.4, para.2A	Police and Criminal Evidence Act 1984, s.32	(a) Objects that might be used to cause physical injury to the person or the CSO (b) Items that might be used to assist escape	Persons made subject to a requirement to wait	Any place where the requirement to wait has been made

3. Powers to seize without consent

This power applies when drugs are found in the course of any search mentioned above.

Designation	Power conferred	Object of seizure	Where Exercisable
Police Reform Act 2002, Sch.4, para.7B	Police Reform Act 2002, Schedule 4, paragraph 7B	Controlled drugs in a person's possession.	Any place where the person is in possession of the drug

CODE B

CODE OF PRACTICE FOR THE SEARCHES OF PREMISES BY POLICE OFFICERS AND THE SEIZURE OF PROPERTY FOUND BY POLICE OFFICERS ON PERSONS OR PREMISES

Commencement—transitional arrangements

Both dates to be changed to read "after midnight on December 31, 2005".

2 General

B 2.11(a). Add "See Note 2G".

B 2.11(c). Add "See Note 3C".

Notes for guidance

B GN 2A(a), p.684, (a) third bullet. Delete "serious arrestable" and insert "an indictable".

B GN 2A(b), p.684. Change to "judge of the High Court, a Circuit judge, a Recorder or a District Judge under"[32].

B GN 2B (a)(i), p.685. Change to "(a) Road Traffic Act 1988, section 6E(1) giving police power to enter premises under section 6E(1) to".

B GN 2B (b), p.685. Remove reference to section 30(3) of the Transport and Works Act 1992.

B GN 2G, p.686. Add GN 2G
"*2G An officer of the rank of inspector or above may direct a designated investigating officer not to wear a uniform for the purposes of a specific operation.*"

3. Search warrants and production orders

(a) Before making an application

B 3.4(a). After "or to a" change to "judge of the High Court, a Circuit judge, a Recorder or a District Judge for a"[33].

---

[32] This flows from a change made by the Courts Act 2003, s.65 and Sch.4, para.6(5) which is not yet in force. Pending implementation of the change, applications under PACE Sch.1 or the Terrorism Act 2000, Sch.5 will continue to be made to a Circuit judge.
[33] See n.32.

(b) Making an application

B 3.6(b). Change to:

"(i) whether the warrant is to authorise entry and search of:
* one set of premises; or
* if the application is under PACE section 8, or Schedule 1, paragraph 12, more than one set of specified premises or all premises occupied or controlled by a specified person, and

(ii) the premises to be searched;"

B 3.6 (d). Add new paras.(da) and (db):

"(da) Where the application is under PACE section 8, or Schedule 1, paragraph 12 for a single warrant to enter and search:

(a) more than one set of specified premises, the officer must specify each set of premises which it is desired to enter and search

(b) all premises occupied or controlled by a specified person, the officer must specify:
* as many sets of premises which it is desired to enter and search as it is reasonably practicable to specify;
* the person who is in occupation or control of those premises and any others which it is desired to search;
* why it is necessary to search more premises than those which can be specified;
* why it is not reasonably practicable to specify all the premises which it is desired to enter and search.

(db) Whether an application under PACE section 8 is for a warrant authorising entry and search on more than one occasion, and if so, the officer must state the grounds for this and whether the desired number of entries authorised is unlimited or a specified maximum."

B 3.6 (e)(i). After "peace or a", change to "judge of the High Court, a Circuit judge, a Recorder or a District Judge"[34]

Notes for guidance

B GN 3B. Final sentence should read *"The meaning of 'items subject to legal privilege', 'excluded material' and 'special procedure material' are defined by PACE sections 10, 11 and 14 respectively."*

---

[34] See n.32.

4 Entry without warrant—particular powers

(b) Search of premises where arrest takes place or the arrested person was immediately before arrest

B 4.2. Replace existing text with "When a person has been arrested for an indictable offence, a police officer has power under PACE, section 32 to search the premises where the person was arrested or where the person was immediately before being arrested."

(c) Search of premises occupied or controlled by the arrested person

B 4.3. Delete "an arrested person" and replace with "a person arrested for an indictable offence"

6 Searching premises—general considerations

(a) Time of searches

B 6.1. Change ". . .one calendar month. . ." to "three calendar months. . ."

B 6.3. Delete "A warrant authorises an entry on one occasion only"

B 6.3A and 6.3B. After 6.3 add new 6.3A and B:
"6.3A A warrant under PACE, section 8 may authorise entry to and search of premises on more than one occasion if, on the application, the justice of the peace is satisfied that it is necessary to authorise multiple entries in order to achieve the purpose for which the warrant is issued. No premises may be entered or searched on any subsequent occasions without the prior written authority of an officer of the rank of inspector who is not involved in the investigation. All other warrants authorise entry on one occasion only.

6.3B Where a warrant under PACE section 8, or Schedule 1, paragraph 12 authorises entry to and search of all premises occupied or controlled by a specified person, no premises which are not specified in the warrant may be entered and searched without the prior written authority of an officer of the rank of inspector who is not involved in the investigation."

8 Action after Searches

B 8.2. At start change to "On each occasion when. . ., the warrant authorising the search on that occasion. . ."

(i) **add at end ". . .** and the address where found"

(iii) **add at end ". . .** and if present, the name of the occupier or if the occupier is not present the name of the person in charge of the premises;"

B 8.3. Change to ". . . three calendar months of its issue or sooner on completion of the search(es) authorised by that warrant. . ."

After "to the", change first bullet to ". . .designated officer for the local justice area in which the justice was acting when issuing the warrant; or"

CODE C

CODE OF PRACTICE FOR THE DETENTION, TREATMENT AND QUESTIONING OF PERSONS BY POLICE OFFICERS

Commencement—Transitional Arrangements

Change to ". . . after midnight on December 31, 2005. . ."

1 General

C 1.9. Delete "those performing the functions of a custody officer." and insert "any:

- police officer; or

- designated staff custody officer acting in the exercise or performance of the powers and duties conferred or imposed on them by their designation,

performing the functions of a custody officer. See Note 1J."

C 1.14. Delete and replace with:
"Designated persons are entitled to use reasonable force as follows:

(a) when exercising a power conferred on them which allows a police officer exercising that power to use reasonable force, a designated person has the same entitlement to use force; and

(b) at other times when carrying out duties conferred or imposed on them that also entitle them to use reasonable force, for example:
  - when at a police station carrying out the duty to keep detainees for whom they are responsible under control and to assist any other police officer or designated person to keep any detainee under control and to prevent their escape;
  - when securing, or assisting any other police officer or designated person in securing, the detention of a person at a police station;
  - when escorting, or assisting any other police officer or designated person in escorting, a detainee within a police station;
  - for the purpose of saving life or limb; or
  - preventing serious damage to property."

Notes for guidance

C GN 1E. Insert at end of paragraph, "*An appropriate adult is not subject to legal privilege.*"

C GN 1J. Add new Notes 1J and 1K:

"*1J   The designation of police staff custody officers applies only in police areas where an order commencing the provisions of the Police Reform Act 2002, section 38 and Schedule 4A, for designating police staff custody officers is in effect.*

1K   This Code does not affect the principle that all citizens have a duty to help police officers to prevent crime and discover offenders. This is a civic rather than a legal duty; but when a police officer is trying to discover whether, or by whom, an offence has been committed he is entitled to question any person from whom he thinks useful information can be obtained, subject to the restrictions imposed by this Code. A person's declaration that he is unwilling to reply does not alter this entitlement."

3 Initial action

(a) Detained persons—normal procedure

C 3.4. Add bullet point at beginning of the list:

* "record the offence(s) that the detainee has been arrested for and the reason(s) for the arrest on the custody record. See paragraph 10.3 and Code G paragraphs 2.2 and 4.3."

(b) Detained persons—special groups

C 3.16. After "imperative" insert "that".

(c) Persons attending a police station voluntarily

C 3.21. After first sentence add "See Note 1K".

Notes for guidance

C GN 3D, 3ʳᵈ bullet. After "*taking fingerprints*" insert ", *footwear impressions. . .*".

4 Detainee's property

(a) Action

C 4.1(a)(i). Add new bullet point "remand into police custody on the authority of a court"

5 Right not to be held incommunicado

(a) Action

C 5.6. In (a) delete "arrestable or serious arrestable" and substitute "indictable". Delete the three lines after sun-para.(b) and substitute: "Nothing in this paragraph permits the restriction or denial of the rights in paras 5.1 or 6.1."

C 5.7A. After para.5.7 insert new para.5.7A:

"5.7A Any delay or denial of the rights in this section should be proportionate and should last no longer than necessary."

6 Right to legal advice

(a) Action

C 6.5. After "16.4" insert ", 2B of Annex A, 3 of Annex K".

C 6.6(d)(i). Change to: "(i) the detainee agrees to do so, in writing or on the interview record made in accordance with Code E or F; and".

C 6.6(d) second para, line 2. Change to: ". . .name of the authorising officer shall be recorded in the written interview record or the interview record made in accordance with Code E or F. See Note 61"

9 Care and treatment of detained persons

(a) General

C 9.3, line 4. After ". . . drugs," insert "or having swallowed drugs, see Note 9CA. . ."

(b) Clinical treatment and attention

C 9.10, line 2. Before "controlled drugs. . ." add "medically prescribed" and delete "1" after "Schedule".

Notes for guidance

C GN 9CA. Insert new Note 9CA:
"*9CA   Paragraph 9.3 would apply to a person in police custody by order of a magistrates' court under the Criminal Justice Act 1988, section 152 (as amended by the Drugs Act 2005, section 8) to facilitate the recovery of evidence after being charged with drug possession or drug trafficking and suspected of having swallowed drugs. In the case of the healthcare needs of a person who has swallowed drugs, the custody officer subject to any clinical directions, should consider the necessity for rousing every half hour. This does not negate the need for regular visiting of the suspect in the cell.*"

10 Cautions

(a) When a caution must be given

C 10.3. At the end of the paragraph change to "see paragraph 3.4, Note 10B and Code G, paragraphs 2.2. and 4.3"

C 10.4. Start paragraph "As per Code G, section 3, a person"

Notes for guidance

C GN 10B. Delete penultimate sentence and substitute: "The suspect must also be informed of the reason or reasons why the arrest is necessary."

12 Interviews in police stations

Notes for guidance

C GN 12A. Change first sentence to: "*12A It is not normally necessary to ask for a written statement if the interview was recorded in writing and the record signed in accordance with paragraph 11.11 or audibly or visually recorded in accordance with Code E or F.*"

13 Interpreters

(a) General

C 13.1. In the last sentence add at end, "or the Council for the Advancement of Communication with Deaf People (CADCP) Directory of British Sign Language/English interpreters."

(b) Foreign languages

C.13.3. Change the last sentence to: "If the interview is audibly recorded or visually recorded, the arrangements in Code E or F apply".

(c) Deaf people and people with speech difficulties

C 13.7. In the second sentence, replace "tape" with "audibly".

(d) Additional rules for detained persons

C 13.9. In the last sentence, replace "tape" with audibly".

15 Reviews and extensions of detention

(a) Persons detained under PACE

C 15.2A. Change "arrestable" to "indictable".

Notes for guidance

C GN 15B(a). Delete *"or failed to answer Street Bail"*.

C GN 15B(g). Insert new (g):

"(g)   detained by order of a magistrates' court under the Criminal Justice Act 1988, section 152 (as amended by the Drugs Act 2005, section 8) to facilitate the recovery of evidence after being charged with drug possession or drug trafficking and suspected of having swallowed drugs."

16 Charging detained persons

(a) Action

C 16.1. At end of paragraph add "s" to "Note".

C 16.1A. Change "Note 16AB" to "Notes 16AA and 16AB".

(b) Documentation

C 16.9. In the second sentence, replace "tape" with "audibly".

Notes for guidance

C GN 16AA. Add new Guidance Note 16AA:

"16AA   When a person is arrested under the provisions of the Criminal Justice Act 2003 which allow a person to be re-tried after being acquitted of a serious offence which is a qualifying offence specified in Schedule 5 to that Act and not precluded from further prosecution by virtue of section 75(3) of that Act the detention provisions of PACE are modified and make an officer of the rank of superintendent or above who has not been directly involved in the investigation responsible for determining whether the evidence is sufficient to charge."

C GN 16AB, first sentence. Insert "a" before "custody officer" and delete from *"are entitled"* to *"a Duty Prosecutor"* and insert *"who determines in accordance with that Guidance that there is sufficient evidence to charge the detainee, may detain that person for no longer than is reasonably necessary to decide how that person is to be dealt with under PACE, section 37(7)(a) to (d), including, where appropriate, consultation with the Duty Prosecutor. The period is subject to the maximum period of detention before charge determined by PACE, sections 41 to 44."*

17 Testing persons for the presence of specified Class A drugs

C 17.1—17.17. Substantial textual redrafting to reflect changes under the Drugs Act 2005, including renumbering of existing paras.7.1—7.14. The text that follows is the new paras.17.1—17.17:

(a) Action

17.1   This section of Code C applies only in selected police stations in police areas where the provisions for drug testing under section 63B of PACE (as amended by section 5 of the Criminal Justice Act 2003 and section 7 of the Drugs Act 2005) are in force and in respect of which the Secretary of State has given a notification to the relevant chief officer of police that arrangements for the taking of samples have been made. Such a notification will cover either a police area as a whole or particular stations within a police area. The notification indicates whether the testing applies to those arrested or charged or under the age of 18 as the case may be and testing can only take place in respect of the persons so indicated in the notification. Testing cannot be carried out unless the relevant notification has been given and has not been withdrawn. See Note 17F

17.2   A sample of urine or a non-intimate sample may be taken from a person in police detention for the purpose of ascertaining whether he has any specified Class A drug in his body only where they have been brought before the custody officer and:

(a)   either the arrest condition, see paragraph 17.3, or the charge condition, see paragraph 17.4 is met;

(b)   the age condition see paragraph 17.5, is met;

(c)   the notification condition is met in relation to the arrest condition, the charge condition, or the age condition, as the case may be. (Testing on charge and/or arrest must be specifically provided for in the notification for the power to apply. In addition, the fact that testing of under 18s is authorised must be expressly provided for in the notification before the power to test such persons applies.). See paragraph 17.1; and

(d)   a police officer has requested the person concerned to give the sample (the request condition).

17.3   The arrest condition is met where the detainee:

(a)   has been arrested for a trigger offence, see Note 17E, but not charged with that offence; or

(b)   has been arrested for any other offence but not charged with that offence and a police officer of inspector rank or above, who has reasonable grounds for suspecting that their misuse of any specified Class A drug caused or contributed to the offence, has authorised the sample to be taken.

17.4   The charge condition is met where the detainee:

    (a)   has been charged with a trigger offence, or

    (b)   has been charged with any other offence and a police officer of inspector rank or above, who has reasonable grounds for suspecting that the detainee's misuse of any specified Class A drug caused or contributed to the offence, has authorised the sample to be taken.

17.5   The age condition is met where:

    (a)   in the case of a detainee who has been arrested but not charged as in paragraph 17.3, they are aged 18 or over;

    (b)   in the case of a detainee who has been charged as in paragraph 17.4, they are aged 14 or over.

17.6   Before requesting a sample from the person concerned, an officer must:

    (a)   inform them that the purpose of taking the sample is for drug testing under PACE. This is to ascertain whether they have a specified Class A drug present in their body;

    (b)   warn them that if, when so requested, they fail without good cause to provide a sample they may be liable to prosecution;

    (c)   where the taking of the sample has been authorised by an inspector or above in accordance with paragraph 17.3(b) or 17.4(b) above, inform them that the authorisation has been given and the grounds for giving it;

    (d)   remind them of the following rights, which may be exercised at any stage during the period in custody:

       (i)   the right to have someone informed of their arrest [see section 5];
      (ii)   the right to consult privately with a solicitor and that free independent legal advice is available [see section 6]; and
     (iii)   the right to consult these Codes of Practice [see section 3].

17.7   In the case of a person who has not attained the age of 17—

    (a)   the making of the request for a sample under paragraph 17.2(d) above;

    (b)   the giving of the warning and the information under paragraph 17.6 above;

and

(c)   the taking of the sample,

may not take place except in the presence of an appropriate adult (see Note 17G).

17.8   Authorisation by an officer of the rank of inspector or above within paragraph 17.3(b) or 17.4(b) may be given orally or in writing but, if it is given orally, it must be confirmed in writing as soon as practicable.

17.9   If a sample is taken from a detainee who has been arrested for an offence but not charged with that offence as in paragraph 17.3, no further sample may be taken during the same continuous period of detention. If during that same period the charge condition is also met in respect of that detainee, the sample which has been taken shall be treated as being taken by virtue of the charge condition, see paragraph 17.4, being met.

17.10   A detainee from whom a sample may be taken may be detained for up to six hours from the time of charge if the custody officer reasonably believes the detention is necessary to enable a sample to be taken. Where the arrest condition is met, a detainee whom the custody officer has decided to release on bail without charge may continue to be detained, but not beyond 24 hours from the relevant time (as defined in section 41(2) of PACE), to enable a sample to be taken.

17.11   A detainee in respect of whom the arrest condition is met, but not the charge condition, see paragraphs 17.3 and 17.4, and whose release would be required before a sample can be taken had they not continued to be detained as a result of being arrested for a further offence which does not satisfy the arrest condition, may have a sample taken at any time within 24 hours after the arrest for the offence that satisfies the arrest condition.

(b) Documentation

17.12   The following must be recorded in the custody record:

(a)   if a sample is taken following authorisation by an officer of the rank of inspector or above, the authorisation and the grounds for suspicion;

(b)   the giving of a warning of the consequences of failure to provide a sample;

(c)   the time at which the sample was given; and

(d)   the time of charge or, where the arrest condition is being relied upon, the time of arrest and, where applicable, the fact that a sample taken after arrest but before charge is to be treated as being taken by virtue of the charge condition, where that is met in the same period of continuous detention. See paragraph 17.9

(c) General

17.13   A sample may only be taken by a prescribed person. See Note 17C.

17.14   Force may not be used to take any sample for the purpose of drug testing.

17.15   The terms "Class A drug" and "misuse" have the same meanings as in the Misuse of Drugs Act 1971. "Specified" (in relation to a Class A drug) and "trigger offence" have the same meanings as in Part III of the Criminal Justice and Court Services Act 2000.

17.16   Any sample taken:

(a)   may not be used for any purpose other than to ascertain whether the person concerned has a specified Class A drug present in his body; and

(b)   must be retained until the person concerned has made their first appearance before the court.[35]

(d) Assessment of misuse of drugs

17.17   Under the provisions of Part 3 of the Drugs Act 2005, where a detainee has tested positive for a specified Class A drug under section 63B of PACE a police officer may, at any time before the person's release from the police station, impose a requirement for them to attend an initial assessment of their drug misuse by a suitably qualified person and to remain for its duration. The requirement may only be imposed on a person if:

(a)   they have reached the age of 18

(b)   notification has been given by the Secretary of State to the relevant chief officer of police that arrangements for conducting initial assessments have been made for those from whom samples for testing have been taken at the police station where the detainee is in custody."

17.18   When imposing a requirement to attend an initial assessment the police officer must:

(a)   inform the person of the time and place at which the initial assessment is to will take place;

(b)   explain that this information will be confirmed in writing: and

---

[35] This is no longer appropriate since as from January 1, 2006, testing has been possible on arrest so that the person tested may not be charged. The Home Office Circular 56/2005 issued in December 2005 stated that this paragraph would be corrected in the next revision of the Codes to the effect that a sample can be disposed of as clinical waste unless it is sent for further analysis where the result is disputed or where medication has been taken, or for quality assurance purposes.

(c)   warn the person that he may be liable to prosecution of he fails without good cause to attend the initial assessment and remain for its duration.

17.19   Where a police officer has impose a requirement to attend an initial assessment in accordance with paragraph 17.17, he must, before the person is released from detention, give the person notice in writing which:

(a)   confirms that he is requires to attend and remain for the duration of an initial assessment; and

(b)   confirms the information and repeats the warning referred to in paragraph 17.18.

17.20   The following must be recorded in the custody record:

(a)   that the requirement to attend an initial assessment has been imposed; and

(b)   the information, explanation, warning and notice given in accordance with paragraphs 17.17 and 17.19.

17.21   Where a notice is given in accordance with paragraph 17.19, a police officer can give the person a further notice in writing which informs the person of any change to the time and place at which the initial assessment is to take place and which repeats the warning referred to in paragraph 17.18(c).

17.22   Part 3 of the Drugs Act 2005 also requires police officers to have regard to any guidance issued by the Secretary of State in respect of the assessment provisions.

Notes for guidance

C GN 17A. Change "*17.1*" to "*17.6(b)*"

C GN 17C. Change "*17.11*" to "*17.13*"

C GN 17D. Change "*17.14*" to "*17.16(b)*"

C GN 17E and 17F. Delete and substitute:
   "*17E Trigger offences are:*

   1.   Offences under the following provisions of the Theft Act 1968:
      section 1   (theft)
      section 8   (robbery)

section 9   *(burglary)*
section 10   *(aggravated burglary)*
section 12   *(taking a motor vehicle or other conveyance without authority)*
section 12A   *(aggravated vehicle-taking)*
section 15   *(obtaining property by deception)*
section 22   *(handling stolen goods)*
section 25   *(going equipped for stealing etc.)*

2.   *Offences under the following provisions of the Misuse of Drugs Act 1971, if committed in respect of a specified Class A drug:*
section 4   *(restriction on production and supply of controlled drugs)*
section 5(2)   *(possession of a controlled drug)*
section 5(3)   *(possession of a controlled drug with intent to supply)*

3.   *An offence under section 1(1) of the Criminal Attempts Act 1981 if committed in respect of an offence under any of the following provisions of the Theft Act 1968:*
section 1   *(theft)*
section 8   *(robbery)*
section 9   *(burglary)*
section 15   *(obtaining property by deception)*
section 22   *(handling stolen goods)*

4.   *Offences under the following provisions of the Vagrancy Act 1824:*
section 3   *(begging)*
section 4   *(persistent begging)*

17F The power to take samples is subject to notification by the Secretary of State that appropriate arrangements for the taking of samples have been made for the police area as a whole or for the particular police station concerned for whichever of the following is specified in the notification:

(a)   *persons in respect of whom the arrest condition is met;*

(b)   *persons in respect of whom the charge condition is met;*

(c)   *persons who have not attained the age of 18.*

Note: Notification is treated as having been given for the purposes of the charge condition in relation to a police area, if testing (on charge) under section 63B(2) of PACE was in force immediately before section 7 of the Drugs Act 2005 was brought into force; and for the purposes of the age condition, in relation to a police area or police station, if immediately before that day, notification that arrangements had been made for the taking of samples from persons under the age of 18 (those aged 14–17) had been given and had not been withdrawn."

C GN 17G. Change "*17.5*" to "*17.7*".

In (a), delete "*he is*" and replace with "*they are*".

In (b), after "*social worker of*" insert "*in England*", and after "*local authority*" insert "*or, in Wales, a local authority*".

ANNEX A

INTIMATE AND STRIP SEARCHES

A Intimate search

(a) Action

Paras.2, 2A and 2B. Delete and substitute new text:

"2. Body orifices other than the mouth may be searched only:

(a) if authorised by an officer of inspector rank or above who has reasonable grounds for believing that the person may have concealed on themselves:

    (i) anything which they could and might use to cause physical injury to themselves or others at the station; or

    (ii) a Class A drug which they intended to supply to another or to export;

and the officer has reasonable grounds for believing that an intimate search is the only means of removing those items; and

(b) if the search is under paragraph 2(a)(ii) (a drug offence search), the detainee's appropriate consent has been given in writing.

2A. Before the search begins, a police officer, designated detention officer or staff custody officer, must tell the detainee:

(a) that the authority to carry out the search has been given;

(b) the grounds for giving the authorisation and for believing that the article cannot be removed without an intimate search.

2B. Before a detainee is asked to give appropriate consent to a search under paragraph 2(a)(ii) (a drug offence search) they must be warned that if they refuse without good cause their refusal may harm their case if it comes to trial, see *Note A6*. This warning may be given by a police officer or member of police staff. A detainee who is not legally represented must be reminded of their entitlement to have free legal advice, see Code C, paragraph 6.5, and the reminder noted in the custody record."

(b) Documentation

Para.7. Change first sentence to: "In the case of an intimate search, the following shall be recorded as soon as practicable, in the detainee's custody record."
—After first sentence delete text and substitute:

"(a) for searches under paragraphs 2(a)(i) and (ii);

- the authorisation to carry out the search;
- the grounds for giving the authorisation;
- the grounds for believing the article could not be removed without an intimate search;
- which parts of the detainee's body were searched;
- who carried out the search;
- who was present;
- the result.

(b) for searches under paragraph 2(a)(ii):

- the giving of the warning required by paragraph 2B;
- the fact that the appropriate consent was given or (as the case may be) refused, and if refused, the reason given for the refusal (if any)."

Notes for guidance

C GN A6. Insert new Guidance Note A6:
"A6 In warning a detainee who is asked to consent to an intimate drug offence search, as in paragraph 2B, the following form of words may be used:

"You do not have to allow yourself to be searched, but I must warn you that if you refuse without good cause, your refusal may harm your case if it comes to trial."

ANNEX B

DELAY IN NOTIFYING ARREST OR ALLOWING ACCESS TO LEGAL ADVICE

A Persons detained under PACE

Para.1. Change all references to "a serious arrestable offence" to "an indictable offence".

Para.2. Delete and replace with:
"These rights may also be delayed if the officer has reasonable grounds to believe that:

(i) the person detained for an indictable offence has benefited from their criminal conduct (decided in accordance with Part 2 of the Proceeds of Crime Act 2002); and

(ii) the recovery of the value of the property constituting that benefit will be hindered by the exercise of either right."

B Persons detained under the Terrorism Act 2000

Para.8. Change all references to "a serious arrestable offence" to "an indictable offence".

Para.9, after "believing". Delete and replace with:
"that:

(i) the person detained has benefited from their criminal conduct (decided in accordance with Part 2 of the Proceeds of Crime Act 2002), and

(ii) the recovery of the value of the property constituting that benefit will be hindered by the exercise of either right."

ANNEX I

POLICE AREAS WHERE THE POWER TO TEST PERSONS AGED 18 AND OVER
FOR SPECIFIED CLASS A DRUGS UNDER SECTION 63B OR PACE
HAS BEEN BROUGHT INTO FORCE

Delete and replace with "Not used".

ANNEX J

POLICE AREAS WHERE THE POWER TO TEST PERSONS AGED 14 AND OVER FOR
SPECIFIED CLASS A DRUGS UNDER SECTION 63B OR PACE
(AS AMENDED BY SECTION 5 OF THE CRIMINAL JUSTICE ACT 2003)
HAS BEEN BROUGT INTO FORCE

Delete and replace with "Not used".

Insert new Annex K.

ANNEX K

X-RAYS AND ULTRASOUND SCANS

(a) Action

1. PACE, section 55A allows a person who has been arrested and is in police detention to have an x-ray taken of them or an ultrasound scan to be carried out on them (or both) if:

    (a) authorised by an officer of inspector rank or above who has reasonable grounds for believing that the detainee:

        (i) may have swallowed a Class A drug; and
        (ii) was in possession of that Class A drug with the intention of supplying it to another or to export; and

    (b) the detainee's appropriate consent has been given in writing.

2. Before an x-ray is taken or an ultrasound scan carried out, a police officer, designated detention officer or staff custody officer must tell the detainee:-

    (a) that the authority has been given; and

    (b) the grounds for giving the authorisation.

3. Before a detainee is asked to give appropriate consent to an x-ray or an ultrasound scan, they must be warned that if they refuse without good cause their refusal may harm their case if it comes to trial, see Notes K1 and K2. This warning may be given by a police officer or member of police staff. A detainee who is not legally represented must be reminded of their entitlement to have free legal advice, see Code C, paragraph 6.5, and the reminder noted in the custody record.

4. An x-ray may be taken, or an ultrasound scan may be carried out, only by a registered medical practitioner or registered nurse, and only at a hospital, surgery or other medical premises.

(b) Documentation

5. The following shall be recorded as soon as practicable in the detainee's custody record:

(a)   the authorisation to take the x-ray or carry out the ultrasound scan (or both);

(b)   the grounds for giving the authorisation;

(c)   the giving of the warning required by paragraph 3; and

(d)   the fact that the appropriate consent was given or (as the case may be) refused, and if refused, the reason given for the refusal (if any); and

(e)   if an x-ray is taken or an ultrasound scan carried out:

- where it was taken or carried out
- who took it or carried it out
- who was present
- the result

6. Paragraphs 1.4–1.7 of this Code apply and an appropriate adult should be present when consent is sought to any procedure under this Annex.

Notes for guidance

K1   If authority is given for an x-ray to be taken or an ultrasound scan to be carried out (or both), consideration should be given to asking a registered medical practitioner or registered nurse to explain to the detainee what is involved and to allay any concerns the detainee might have about the effect which taking an x-ray or carrying out an ultrasound scan might have on them. If appropriate consent is not given, evidence of the explanation may, if the case comes to trial, be relevant to determining whether the detainee had a good cause for refusing.

K2   In warning a detainee who is asked to consent to an x-ray being taken or an ultrasound scan being carried out (or both), as in paragraph 3, the following form of words may be used:

"You do not have to allow an x-ray of you to be taken or an ultrasound scan to be carried out on you, but I must warn you that if you refuse without good cause, your refusal may harm your case if it comes to trial."

CODE D

CODE OF PRACTICE FOR THE IDENTIFICATION OF PERSONS BY POLICE OFFICERS

1 Introduction

D 1.3A. Insert new D 1.3A:

"1.3A   Identification using footwear impressions applies when a person's footwear impressions are taken to compare with impressions found at the scene of a crime."

2 General

D 2.7. Add ", see paragraph 1.9 of Code C."

D 2.15. Change to: "Any procedure in this Code involving the participation of a suspect who is mentally disordered, otherwise mentally vulnerable or a juvenile must take place in the presence of the appropriate adult. See Code C paragraph 1.4."

D 2.15A. Insert new 2.15A: "Any procedure in this Code involving the participation of a witness who is or appears to be mentally disordered, otherwise mentally vulnerable or a juvenile should take place in the presence of a pre-trial support person. However, the support-person must not be allowed to prompt any identification of a suspect by a witness. See Note 2AB."

D 2.16, first bullet point, after "still". Insert "or moving".

D 2.21, line 6. Change "civilian" to "person".

Notes for guidance

D after GN 2A. Insert new GN 2AB:

"2AB   The Youth Justice and Criminal Evidence Act 1999 guidance "Achieving Best Evidence in Criminal Proceedings" indicates that a pre-trial support person should accompany a vulnerable witness during any identification procedure. It states that this support person should not be (or not be likely to be) a witness in the investigation."

3 Identification by witnesses

(b) Cases when the suspect is known and available

Video identification

D 3.5. Delete second sentence and replace with:

"Moving images must be used unless:

- the suspect is known but not available (see paragraph 3.21 of this Code); or

- in accordance with paragraph 2A of Annex A of this Code, the identification officer does not consider that replication of a physical feature can be achieved or that it is not possible to conceal the location of the feature on the image of the suspect.

The identification officer may then decide to make use of video identification but using still images."

Notice to suspect

D 3.19 (a) and (b). Change to:

"(a) it is proposed to release the suspect in order that an identification procedure can be arranged and carried out and an inspector is not available to act as the identification officer, see paragraph 3.11, before the suspect leaves the station; or

(b) it is proposed to keep the suspect in police detention whilst the procedure is arranged and carried out and waiting for an inspector to act as the identification officer, see paragraph 3.11, would cause unreasonable delay to the investigation."

(f) Destruction and retention of photographs and images taken or used in identification procedures

D 3.30. Delete "and images" from heading.

D 3.30. After "64A," insert "see paragraph 5.12". Delete "detained at police stations". At the end of first sentence add "or the enforcement of a sentence."

D 3.31. Delete "detained and any moving images, (and copies) of suspects whether or not they have been detained" and replace with "taken in accordance with the provisions in paragraph 5.12."

D 3.32. Remove "or images"

Notes for guidance

D GN 3D. At the end of the paragraph add: *"Examples include images from custody and other CCTV systems and from visually recorded interview records, see Code F Note for Guidance 2D."*

4 Identification by fingerprints

D 4 heading. Add "and footwear impressions".

(A) Taking fingerprints in connection with a criminal investigation

(b) Action

D 4.7 (b). Remove "s" from "powers".

D 4(C). Add new section 4C:

"(C) Taking footwear impressions in connection with a criminal investigation

(a) Action

4.16 Impressions of a person's footwear may be taken in connection with the investigation of an offence only with their consent or if paragraph 4.17 applies. If the person is at a police station consent must be in writing.

4.17 PACE, section 61A, provides power for a police officer to take footwear impressions without consent from any person over the age of ten years who is detained at a police station:

(a) in consequence of being arrested for a recordable offence, see Note 4A; or if the detainee has been charged with a recordable offence, or informed they will be reported for such an offence; and

(b) the detainee has not had an impression of their footwear taken in the course of the investigation of the offence unless the previously taken impression is not complete or is not of sufficient quality to allow satisfactory analysis, comparison or matching (whether in the case in question or generally).

4.18 Reasonable force may be used, if necessary, to take a footwear impression from a detainee without consent under the power in paragraph 4.17.

4.19 Before any footwear impression is taken with, or without, consent as above, the person must be informed:

(a) of the reason the impression is to be taken;

(b) that the impression may be retained and may be subject of a speculative search against other impressions, see Note 4B, unless destruction of the impression is required in accordance with Annex F, Part (a); and

(c) that if their footwear impressions are required to be destroyed, they may witness their destruction as provided for in Annex F, Part (a).

(b) Documentation

4.20 A record must be made as soon as possible, of the reason for taking a person's footwear impressions without consent. If force is used, a record shall be made of the circumstances and those present.

4.21 A record shall be made when a person has been informed under the terms of paragraph 4.19(b), of the possibility that their footwear impressions may be subject of a speculative search."

Notes for guidance

D GN 4A. Line 7, after "*under*" insert "*the Vagrancy Act 1824 sections 3 and 4 (begging and persistent begging),*" and delete "*the Telecommunications Act 1984, section 43 (improper use of public telecommunications systems),*" and "*the Malicious Communications Act 1988, section 1 (sending letters, etc. with intent to cause distress or anxiety)*". After "motor vehicles)", add "*the Criminal Justice and Public Order Act 1994, section 167 (touting for hire car services)*". At the end of the paragraph after 2000, add "*as amended*".

D GN 4B. Wherever the word "*fingerprints*" appears add "*footwear impressions*". In second paragraph of statement delete "*this*" and replace with "*DNA*". In the third paragraph of statement delete "*the*" and replace with "*my fingerprints, footwear impressions or DNA*".

5 Examinations to establish identity and the taking of photographs

(A) Detainees at police stations

(b) Photographing detainees at police stations

D 5. Add "and other persons elsewhere than at a police station" to end of heading.

D 5.12. Replace 5.12 and insert new 5.12A:
"5.12 Under PACE, section 64A, an officer may photograph:

(a) any person whilst they are detained at a police station; and

(b) any person who is elsewhere than at a police station and who has been:
   (i) arrested by a constable for an offence;
   (ii) taken into custody by a constable after being arrested for an offence by a person other than a constable;
   (iii) made subject to a requirement to wait with a community support officer under paragraph 2(3) or (3B) of Schedule 4 to the Police Reform Act 2002;
   (iv) given a penalty notice by a constable in uniform under Chapter 1 of Part 1 of the Criminal Justice and Police Act 2001, a penalty notice by a constable under section 444A of the Education Act 1996, or a fixed penalty notice by a constable in uniform under section 54 of the Road Traffic Offenders Act 1988;
   (v) given a notice in relation to a relevant fixed penalty offence (within the meaning of paragraph 1 of Schedule 4 to the Police Reform Act 2002) by a community support officer by virtue of a designation applying that paragraph to him; or
   (vi) given a notice in relation to a relevant fixed penalty offence (within the meaning of paragraph 1 of Schedule 5 to the Police Reform Act 2002) by an accredited person by virtue of accreditation specifying that that paragraph applies to him."

5.12A Photographs taken under PACE, section 64A:

(a) may be taken with the person's consent, or without their consent if consent is withheld or it is not practicable to obtain their consent, see Note 5E; and

(b) may be used or disclosed only for purposes related to the prevention or detection of crime, the investigation of offences or the conduct of prosecutions by, or on behalf of, police or other law enforcement and prosecuting authorities inside and outside the United Kingdom or the enforcement of any sentence or order made by a court when dealing with an offence. After being so used or disclosed, they may be retained but can only be used or disclosed for the same purposes. See Note 5B."

D 5.14. After "reasonable force", delete semi-colon and add "see Note F".

(B) Persons at police stations not detained

D 5.22. Delete "or images" and "not detained". After "marks" add "which are not taken in accordance with the provisions mentioned in paragraphs 5.1 or 5.12."

D 5.23. Delete "or images".

Notes for guidance

D GN 5F. Add new Note for Guidance 5F:

"5F   The use of reasonable force to take the photograph of a suspect elsewhere than at a police station must be carefully considered. In order to obtain a suspect's consent and co-operation to remove an item of religious headwear to take their photograph, a constable should consider whether in the circumstances of the situation the removal of the headwear and the taking of the photograph should be by an officer of the same sex as the person. It would be appropriate for these actions to be conducted out of public view."

6 Identification by body samples and impressions

(a) General

D 6.1(a). After "a swab taken from" insert "any part of a person's genitals or from".

6.1(b)(iii). After "person's body" insert "other than a part from which a swab taken would be an intimate sample" and delete "including the mouth but not any other body orifice".

ANNEX A

VIDEO IDENTIFICATION

(a) General

D Annex A2, line 2. Delete "height".

D Annex A. Add new paragraphs 2A, 2B and 2C:
"2A   If the suspect has an unusual physical feature, e.g., a facial scar, tattoo or distinctive hairstyle or hair colour which does not appear on the images of the other people that are available to be used, steps may be taken to:

(a)   conceal the location of the feature on the images of the suspect and the other people; or

(b)   replicate that feature on the images of the other people.

For these purposes, the feature may be concealed or replicated electronically or by any other method which it is practicable to use to ensure that the images of the suspect and other people resemble each other. The identification officer has discretion to choose whether to conceal or replicate the feature and the method to be used. If an unusual physical feature has been described by the witness, the identification officer should, if practicable, have that feature replicated. If it has not been described, concealment may be more appropriate.
    2B   If the identification officer decides that a feature should be concealed or replicated, the reason for the decision and whether the feature was concealed or replicated in the images shown to any witness shall be recorded.
    2C   If the witness requests to view an image where an unusual physical feature has been concealed or replicated without the feature being concealed or replicated, the witness may be allowed to do so."

(b) Conducting the video identification

D Annex A, para.10, line 3. After "the case" insert ", see any of the images which are to be shown, see, or be reminded of, any photograph or description of the suspect or be given any other indication as to the suspect's identity,"

Annex F

Fingerprints and Samples—Destruction and Speculative Searches

D Annex F. In title, after "FINGERPRINTS" insert ", FOOTWEAR IMPRESSIONS".

(a) Fingerprints and samples taken in connection with a criminal investigation

D Annex F. In title after "Fingerprints" insert ", footwear impressions".

D Annex F, paras.1 to 4. After each reference to "fingerprints" insert ", footwear impressions", except for 3(a) which should be followed by "and footwear impressions".

Notes for guidance

D GN F1. After every reference to "fingerprints" insert ", footwear impressions". In the third sentence delete "sample or" and add "or samples" after ", footwear impressions". After bullet points, at the end of the paragraph delete "one or the other, not both" and substitute "each consent". Change all references to "screen" to "screening".

D GN F1(c). Insert new Note for Guidance:
"(c) Footwear impressions:

    (i) Footwear impressions taken for the purposes of elimination or as part of an intelligence-led screening and to be used only for the purposes of that investigation and destroyed afterwards:

    I consent to my footwear impressions being taken for elimination purposes. I understand that the footwear impressions will be destroyed at the end of the case and that my footwear impressions will only be compared to the footwear impressions from this enquiry. I have been advised that the person taking the footwear impressions may be required to give evidence and/or provide a written statement to the police in relation to the taking of it.

    (ii) Footwear impressions to be retained for future use:

    I consent to my footwear impressions being retained and used only for purposes related to the prevention and detection of a crime, the investigation of an offence or the conduct of a prosecution, either nationally or internationally.

I understand that my footwear impressions may be checked against other records held by, or on behalf of, relevant law enforcement authorities, either nationally or internationally.
I understand that once I have given my consent for my footwear impressions to be retained and used I cannot withdraw this consent.

D GN F2. After every reference to "fingerprints" insert ", footwear impressions".

CODE E

CODE OF PRACTICE ON TAPE RECORDING INTERVIEWS WITH SUSPECTS

Title. Delete "tape" and insert "audio".

Commencement—Transitional arrangements

Change to "December 31, 2005".

1 General

E 1.6. Insert new definition (aa):

"(aa) 'recording media' means any removable, physical audio recording medium (such as magnetic tape, optical disc or solid state memory) which can be played or copied".

E 1.11 at end. Add "as in paragraph 1.9 of Code C".

2 Recording and sealing master tapes

E 2. Change references to "tapes" or "tape" to "recordings" or "recording" and after "deck" insert "/drive".

E 2.1. Change "Tape recording" to "Recording".

Notes for guidance

E GN 2B. Delete text and replace with "Not used".

3 Interviews to be tape recorded

E 3 Title. Delete "tape" and replace with "audio".

E3. Through out the section replace "tape" with "audio".

4 The interview

(b) Commencement of interviews

E 4.3. Change "clean tapes" to "new recording media". In final sentence replace "tapes" with "recording media".

E 4.4. Change to: "The interviewer should tell the suspect about the recording process".

E 4.4(a). Replace "tape" with "audibly".

E 4.4(e). Replace "tapes" with "copies of the recording".

(c) Interviews with deaf persons

E 4.7. Replace "tape" with "audio".

(d) Objections and complaints by the suspect

E 4.8. In the first sentence replace "tape" with "audibly" and replace the end of the sentence from "suspects" with "objections to be recorded on the audio recording". In the final sentence replace "tape" with "audio recording". Add new sentence at the end: "This procedure also applies in cases where the suspect has previously objected to the interview being visually recorded, see Code F 4.8 and the investigating officer has decided to audibly record the interview. See Note 4D."

E 4.10. Replace "tape" with "audio".

(e) Changing tapes

Title. Delete "tapes" and replace with "recording media".

E 4.11. Delete first sentence and substitute: "When the recorder shows the recording media only has a short time left, the interviewer shall tell the suspect the recording media are coming to an end and round off that part of the interview. If the interviewer leaves the room for a second set of recording media, the suspect shall not be left unattended." In the second and third sentences change "tapes" to "recording media" or "media" and change references to "tape recorder" to "recorder". In the third sentence after "immediately" insert "after".

(f) Taking a break during interview

E 4.12. Delete "tape" and replace with "the audio recording".

E4.12A. Delete "tapes" and replace with "recording media" and change reference to "tape recorder" to "recorder".

E 4.13. After "interview room" change to "the recording may be stopped. There is no need to remove the recording media and when the interview recommences the recording should continue on the same recording media. The time the interview recommences shall be recorded on the audio recording."

(g) Failure of recording equipment

E 4.15. Delete "tapes" and replace with "recording media", change reference to "tape recorder" to "recorder" and change "tape recorded" to "audibly recorded".

(h) Removing tapes from the recorder

Title. Delete "tapes" and replace with "recording media".

E 4.16. Delete "tapes" and replace with "recording media". Change "are" to "is".

(i) Conclusion of interview

E 4.18. After "shall be recorded and", change to "the recording shall be stopped. The interviewer shall seal the master recording with a master recording label".

E 4.19. In first bullet change "tape" to "audio". In third bullet change "tape" to "audio recording".

Notes for guidance

E GN 4C. Change "*a tape recorded interview*" to "*an audibly recorded interview*".

E GN 4E. Delete "*tape*".

E GN 4G. Change the last sentence to "*the interviewer should consider summarising on the record the reason for the break and confirming with the suspect.*"

E GN 4H. Delete and replace with:

"*4H   Where the interview is being recorded and the media or the recording equipment fails the officer conducting the interview should stop the interview immediately. Where part of the interview is unaffected by the error and is still accessible on the media, that media shall be copied and sealed in the suspect's presence and the interview recommenced using new equipment/media as required. Where the content of the interview has been lost in its entirety the media should be sealed in the suspect's presence and the interview begun again. If the recording equipment cannot be fixed or no replacement is immediately available the interview should be recorded in accordance with Code C, section 11.*"

5 After the interview

E 5.1. After "taken place", change to "was audibly recorded, its time, duration and date and the master recording's identification number".

E 5.2. Delete "tapes" and replace with "recording media".

Note for guidance

E GN 5A. Change "a tape recorded" to "an audibly recorded".

6 Tape security

E 6 Title. Delete "Tape" and replace with "Media".

E 6. Change references to "tapes" or "tape" to "recordings" or "recording".

Notes for guidance

E GN 6C. Delete "tape" and replace with "audibly".

CODE F

CODE OF PRACTICE ON VISUAL RECORDING WITH SOUND OF INTERVIEWS WITH SUSPECTS

Commencement

After "with a suspect" add "after midnight on October 31, 2005". Delete "1 August 2004".

Notes for guidance

F GN 1A. Insert at start "*As in paragraph 1.9 of Code C,*".

F GN 2D. Delete "*is not to*" and insert "*may*" and change "*any identification purpose*" to "*identification procedures in accordance with paragraph 3.21 or Annex E of Code D.*"

4 The Interview

(a) General

F 4.2. Remove "s" from "determines".

(d) Objections and complaints by the suspect

F 4.8. At the end of the first sentence insert "on the visual recording". Delete "The suspect's objections shall be noted." and insert:
"When any objections have been visually recorded or the suspect has refused to have their objections recorded, the interviewer shall say that they are turning off the recording equipment, give their reasons and turn it off. If a separate audio recording is being maintained, the officer shall ask the person to record the reasons for refusing to agree to visual recording of the interview. Paragraph 4.8 of Code E will apply if the person objects to audio recording of the interview. The officer shall then make a written record of the interview. If the interviewer reasonably considers they may proceed to question the suspect with the visual recording still on, the interviewer may do so. See Note 4G."

Notes for guidance

F GN 4G. Insert new Guidance Note:
"*4G The interviewer should be aware that a decision to continue recording against the wishes of the suspect may be the subject of comment in court.*"

6 Tape Security

F 6. Change title to "Master Copy Security".

After Code F insert new Code G:

CODE G

CODE OF PRACTICE FOR THE STATUTORY POWER OF ARREST BY POLICE OFFICERS

Commencement

This Code applies to any arrest made by a police officer after midnight on December 31, 2005.

1 Introduction

1.1 This Code of Practice deals with statutory power of police to arrest persons suspected of involvement in a criminal offence.

1.2 The right to liberty is a key principle of the Human Rights Act 1998. The exercise of the power of arrest represents an obvious and significant interference with that right.

1.3 The use of the power must be fully justified and officers exercising the power should consider if the necessary objectives can be met by other, less intrusive means. Arrest must never be used simply because it can be used. Absence of justification for exercising the power of arrest may lead to challenges should the case proceed to court. When the power of arrest is exercised it is essential that it is exercised in a non-discriminatory and proportionate manner.

1.4 Section 24 of the Police and Criminal Evidence Act 1984 (as substituted by section 110 of the Serious Organised Crime and Police Act 2005) provides the statutory power of arrest. If the provisions of the Act and this Code are not observed, both the arrest and the conduct of any subsequent investigation may be open to question.

1.5 This code of practice must be readily available at all police stations for consultation by police officers and police staff, detained persons and members of the public.

1.6 The notes for guidance are not provisions of this code.

2 Elements of Arrest under section 24 PACE

2.1 A lawful arrest requires two elements:

A person's involvement or suspected involvement or attempted involvement in the commission of a criminal offence;

AND

Reasonable grounds for believing that the person's arrest is necessary.

2.2 Arresting officers are required to inform the person arrested that they have been arrested, even if this fact is obvious, and of the relevant circumstances of the arrest in relation to both elements and to inform the custody officer of these on arrival at the police station. See Code C paragraph 3.4.

'Involvement in the commission of an offence'

2.3 A constable may arrest without warrant in relation to any offence, except for the single exception listed in Note for Guidance 1. A constable may arrest anyone:

- who is about to commit an offence or is in the act of committing an offence

- whom the officer has reasonable grounds for suspecting is about to commit an offence or to be committing an offence

- whom the officer has reasonable grounds to suspect of being guilty of an offence which he or she has reasonable grounds for suspecting has been committed

- anyone who is guilty of an offence which has been committed or anyone whom the officer has reasonable grounds for suspecting to be guilty of that offence.

Necessity criteria

2.4 The power of arrest is only exercisable if the constable has reasonable grounds for believing that it is necessary to arrest the person. The criteria for what may constitute necessity are set out in paragraph 2.9. It remains an operational decision at the discretion of the arresting officer as to:

- what action he or she may take at the point of contact with the individual;

- the necessity criterion or criteria (if any) which applies to the individual; and

- whether to arrest, report for summons, grant street bail, issue a fixed penalty notice or take any other action that is open to the officer.

2.5 In applying the criteria, the arresting officer has to be satisfied that at least one of the reasons supporting the need for arrest is satisfied.

2.6 Extending the power of arrest to all offences provides a constable with the ability to use that power to deal with any situation. However applying the necessity criteria requires the constable to examine and justify the reason or reasons why a person needs to be taken to a police station for the custody officer to decide whether the person should be placed in police detention.

2.7 The criteria below are set out in section 24 of PACE as substituted by section 110 of the Serious Organised Crime and Police Act 2005. The criteria are exhaustive. However, the circumstances that may satisfy those criteria remain a matter for the operational discretion of individual officers. Some examples are given below of what those circumstances may be.

2.8 In considering the individual circumstances, the constable must take into account the situation of the victim, the nature of the offence, the circumstances of the offender and the needs of the investigative process.

2.9 The criteria are that the arrest is necessary:

(a)　to enable the name of the person in question to be ascertained (in the case where the constable does not know, and cannot readily ascertain, the person's name, or has reasonable grounds for doubting whether a name given by the person as his name is his real name)

(b)　correspondingly as regards the person's address:

an address is a satisfactory address for service of summons if the person will be at it for a sufficiently long period for it to be possible to serve him or her with a summons; or, that some other person at that address specified by the person will accept service of the summons on their behalf.

(c)　to prevent the person in question:
(i)　causing physical injury to himself or any other person;
(ii)　suffering physical injury ;
(iii)　causing loss or damage to property;
(iv)　committing an offence against public decency (only applies where members of the public going about their normal business cannot reasonably be expected to avoid the person in question); or
(v)　causing an unlawful obstruction of the highway;

(d)　to protect a child or other vulnerable person from the person in question,

(e)　to allow the prompt and effective investigation of the offence or of the conduct of the person in question.

This may include cases such as:

(i)　Where there are grounds to believe that the person:
- has made false statements;
- has made statements which cannot be readily verified;
- has presented false evidence;
- may steal or destroy evidence;

- may make contact with co-suspects or conspirators;
- may intimidate or threaten or make contact with witnesses;
- when it is necessary to obtain evidence by questioning; or

(ii) when considering arrest in connection with an indictable offence, there is a need to:

- enter and search any premises occupied or controlled by a person
- search the person
- prevent contact with others
- take fingerprints, footwear impressions, samples or photographs of the suspect

(iii) ensuring compliance with statutory drug testing requirements.

(f) to prevent any prosecution for the offence from being hindered by the disappearance of the person in question.

This may arise if there are reasonable grounds for believing that.

- if the person is not arrested he or she will fail to attend court
- street bail after arrest would be sufficient to deter the suspect from trying to evade prosecution

3 Information to be given on Arrest

(a) Cautions—when a caution must be given (taken from Code C section 10)

3.1 A person whom there are grounds to suspect of an offence (see Note 2) must be cautioned before any questions about an offence, or further questions if the answers provide the grounds for suspicion, are put to them if either the suspect's answers or silence, (i.e. failure or refusal to answer or answer satisfactorily) may be given in evidence to a court in a prosecution. A person need not be cautioned if questions are for other necessary purposes e.g.:

(a) solely to establish their identity or ownership of any vehicle;

(b) to obtain information in accordance with any relevant statutory requirement;

(c) in furtherance of the proper and effective conduct of a search, e.g. to determine the need to search in the exercise of powers of stop and search or to seek co-operation while carrying out a search;

(d) to seek verification of a written record as in Code C paragraph 11.13;

(e) when examining a person in accordance with the Terrorism Act 2000, Schedule 7 and the Code of Practice for Examining Officers issued under that Act, Schedule 14, paragraph 6.

3.2 Whenever a person not under arrest is initially cautioned, or reminded they are under caution, that person must at the same time be told they are not under arrest and are free to leave if they want to.

3.3 A person who is arrested, or further arrested, must be informed at the time, or as soon as practicable thereafter, that they are under arrest and the grounds for their arrest, see *Note 3*.

3.4 A person who is arrested, or further arrested, must also be cautioned unless:

(a)   it is impracticable to do so by reason of their condition or behaviour at the time;

(b)   they have already been cautioned immediately prior to arrest as in paragraph 3.1.

(c)   Terms of the caution (Taken from Code C, section 10)

3.5 The caution, which must be given on arrest, should be in the following terms: "You do not have to say anything. But it may harm your defence if you do not mention when questioned something which you later rely on in Court. Anything you do say may be given in evidence." See Note 5.

3.6 Minor deviations from the words of any caution given in accordance with this Code do not constitute a breach of this Code, provided the sense of the relevant caution is preserved. See Note 6.

3.7 When, despite being cautioned, a person fails to co-operate or to answer particular questions which may affect their immediate treatment, the person should be informed of any relevant consequences and that those consequences are not affected by the caution. Examples are when a person's refusal to provide:

- their name and address when charged may make them liable to detention;

- particulars and information in accordance with a statutory requirement, e.g. under the Road Traffic Act 1988, may amount to an offence or may make the person liable to a further arrest.

4 Records of Arrest

(a) General

4.1 The arresting officer is required to record in his pocket book or by other methods used for recording information:

- the nature and circumstances of the offence leading to the arrest;

- the reason or reasons why arrest was necessary;

- the giving of the caution;

- anything said by the person at the time of arrest.

4.2 Such a record should be made at the time of the arrest unless impracticable to do. If not made at that time, the record should then be completed as soon as possible thereafter.

4.3 On arrival at the police station, the custody officer shall open the custody record (see paragraph 1.1A and section 2 of Code C). The information given by the arresting officer on the circumstances and reason or reasons for arrest shall be recorded as part of the custody record. Alternatively, a copy of the record made by the officer in accordance with paragraph 4.1 above shall be attached as part of the custody record.

4.4 The custody record will serve as a record of the arrest. Copies of the custody record will be provided in accordance with paragraphs 2.4 and 2.4A of Code C and access for inspection of the original record in accordance with paragraph 2.5 of Code C.

(b) Interviews and arrests

4.5 Records of interview, significant statements or silences will be treated in the same way as set out in sections 10 and 11 of Code C and in Code E (tape recording of interviews).

Notes for guidance

1 The powers of arrest for offences under sections 4(1) and 5(1) of the Criminal Law Act 1967 require that the offences to which they relate must carry a sentence fixed by law or one in which a first time offender aged 18 or over could be sentenced to five years' or more imprisonment.

2 There must be some reasonable, objective grounds for the suspicion, based on known facts or information which are relevant to the likelihood the offence has been committed and the person to be questioned committed it.

3 An arrested person must be given sufficient information to enable them to understand they have been deprived of their liberty and the reason they have been arrested, e.g. when a person is arrested on suspicion of committing an offence they must be informed of the suspected offence's nature, when and where it was committed. The suspect must also be informed of the reason or reasons why arrest is considered necessary. Vague or technical language should be avoided.

4 Nothing in this Code requires a caution to be given or repeated when informing a person not under arrest they may be prosecuted for an offence. However, a court will not be able to draw any inferences under the Criminal Justice and Public Order Act 1994, section 34, if the person was not cautioned.

5 If it appears a person does not understand the caution, the people giving it should explain it in their own words.

6 The powers available to an officer as the result of an arrest—for example, entry and search of premises, holding a person incommunicado, setting up road blocks—are only available in respect of indictable offences and are subject to the specific requirements on authorisation as set out in the 1984 Act and relevant PACE Code of Practice.

NOTICE OF RIGHTS AND ENTITLEMENTS

Code C, para.3.2 recites that the things that must be given to suspects include a note "briefly setting out their entitlements while in custody". Code C, Note 3A specifies some of the matters that should be included in the notice of entitlements. Note 3B adds that it should be available in languages other than English. (It is now available on the Home Office PACE website in no fewer than 43 languages!)

The text of the Notice of Rights and Entitlements as amended by the 2006 revision of the Codes is as follows:

The following rights and entitlements are guaranteed to you under the law in England and Wales and comply with the European Convention on Human Rights.

You will find more details about these rights inside.

Remember your rights:

1. **Tell the police if you want a solicitor to help you while you are at the police station. It is free.**

2. **Tell the police if you want someone to be told that you are at the police station. It is free.**

3. **Tell the police if you want to look at their rule-book called the Codes of Practice.**

More information for people arrested by the police

Please keep this information and read it as soon as possible. It will help you to make decisions while you are at the police station.

1. Getting a solicitor to help you

- A solicitor can help and advise you about the law.

- If you want a solicitor, tell the police custody officer. The police will help you get in touch with a solicitor for you.

- The police must let you talk to a solicitor at any time, day or night, when you are at a police station. It is free.

- If you do not know of a solicitor in the area or you cannot get in touch with your own solicitor, you can speak to the duty solicitor. It is free. The police will help you contact him or her for you. The duty solicitor is nothing to do with the police.

- You are entitled to a private consultation with your solicitor on the telephone or they may decide to come and see you at the police station.

- Usually, the police are not allowed to ask you questions until you have had the chance to talk to a solicitor. When the police ask you questions you can ask for a solicitor to be in the room with you.

- If you ask to speak to a solicitor it does not make it look like you have done anything wrong.

- If a solicitor does not turn up, or you need to talk to a solicitor again, ask the police to contact him or her again.

- If you tell the police that you don't want to speak to a solicitor but then you change your mind, tell the police custody officer. The police will then help you contact a solicitor for you.

If you are asked questions about a suspected offence, you do not have to say anything. However, it may harm your defence if you do not mention when questioned something which you later rely on in court. Anything you do say may be given in evidence.

2. Telling someone that you are at the police station

You can ask the police to contact someone to inform them that you are at the police station. It is free. They will contact someone for you as soon as they can.

3. Looking at the Codes of Practice

- The Codes of Practice is a book that tells you what the police can and cannot do while you are at the police station.

- The police will let you read the Codes of Practice but you cannot read it for so long that it holds up the police finding out if you have broken the law.

- If you want to read the Codes of Practice, tell the police custody officer.

Getting details of your time at the police station

- Everything that happens to you when you are at the police station is put on paper and is called the custody record.

- When you leave the police station, you, your solicitor or your appropriate adult can ask for a copy of the custody record. The police have to give you a copy of the custody record as soon as they can.

- You can ask the police for a copy of the custody record up to 12 months after you leave the police station.

How you should be cared for

These are short notes about what you can expect while you are kept at the police station. To find out more, ask to see the book called the Codes of Practice. Inside its back cover you will find a list of where to find more information about each of these things. Ask the police custody officer if you have any questions.

Keeping in touch

As well as talking to a solicitor and having a person told about your arrest you will usually be allowed to make one phone call. Ask the police if you would like to make a phone call. You can also ask for a pen and paper. You may be able to have visitors but the custody officer can refuse to allow that.

Your cell

If possible you should be kept in a cell on your own. It should be clean, warm and lit. Your bedding should be clean and in good order. You must be allowed to use a toilet and have a wash.

Clothes

If your own clothes are taken from you, then the police must provide you with an alternative form of clothing.

Food and drink

You must be offered three meals a day with drinks. You can also have drinks between meals.

Exercise

If possible you should be allowed outside each day for fresh air.

If you are unwell

Ask to see a doctor if you feel ill or need medicine. The police will call a doctor for you and it is free. You can ask to see another doctor but you may have to pay for this. You may be allowed to take your own medicine but the police will have to check with a doctor first. A nurse may see you first, but they will send for a doctor if you need one.

How long can you be detained?

You can normally be detained for up to 24 hours without being charged. This can be longer but only if a Police Superintendent allows it to happen. After 36 hours only a court can allow more time without you being charged. Every so often a senior police officer has to look into your case to see if you should still be kept here. This is called a review. You have the right to have your say about this decision, unless you are not in a fit state.

When the police question you

- The room should be clean, warm and lit.

- You should not have to stand up.

- The police officers should tell you their name and their rank.

- You should have a break at normal meal times and a break for a drink after about two hours.

- You should be allowed at least eight hours rest in any 24 hours you are in custody.

People who need help

- If you are under 17, or you have learning problems or a mental problem then you should have someone with you when the police do certain things. This person is called your "appropriate adult".

- Your appropriate adult must be with you when the police tell you about your rights and tell you why you are being kept at the police station. He or she must also be with you when the police read the police caution to you. He or she must also be with you if you are interviewed.

- The police might also need to do one of the things listed below while you are at the police station. Your appropriate adult should be with you for the whole time if the police do any of these things:

  - Interview you or ask you to sign a written statement or police notes.
  - Review your case.
  - Remove more than your outer clothes.
  - Carry out anything about an identification parade.
  - Charge you with an offence.

You can speak to your solicitor without your appropriate adult in the room if you want.

Breath tests

If you are under arrest because of a drink drive offence, you have the right to speak to a solicitor. That right does not mean you can refuse to give the police samples of breath, blood or urine even if you have not yet spoken to the solicitor.

Independent custody visitors

There are members of the community who are allowed access to police stations unannounced. They are known as independent custody visitors and work on a voluntary basis to make sure that detained people are being treated properly and have access to rights. You do not have a right to see an independent custody visitor and cannot request that an independent custody visitor visit you. If an independent custody visitor does visit you while you are in custody they will be acting independently of the police to check that your welfare and rights have been protected. However, you do not have to speak to them if you do not wish to.

INDEX

Note—Roman type is used to indicate pages in the Commentary, **bold** type to indicate sections of the Police and Criminal Evidence Act 1984, the Drugs Act 2005 and the Police Reform Act 2002 and *italic* type to indicate paragraphs in the Codes of Practice (A to G). The abbreviation A, B, C, D, E, F, G, stands for Code A, Code B etc. The abbreviation *N* stands for Note for Guidance.